MONSTERS WHO

MURDER

SERIAL KILLER CONFESSIONS

AMANDA HOWARD

K

KILLING TIME BOOKS

Printed in USA
ISBN: 978-1727559484
Killing Time Books
NSW Australia
www.amandahoward.com.au

MONSTERS

WHO

MURDER

SERIAL KILLER CONFESSIONS

AMANDA HOWARD

Books by the author

Contents

David and Catherine Birnie

David Birnie was born in 1951 in Wattle Grove, Australia, to alcoholic parents. He was the eldest of five children. After ten years of the children being repeatedly removed from their parents due to neglect, all five Birnie children were sent to different foster homes. Some of them lost contact forever. Later, Birnie contemplated what the rest of his siblings must have thought of him as one of the country's worst killers. He felt as though he were an embarrassment.

Catherine was born Catherine Margaret Harrison[1] and never knew her mother, who died when she was less than two years old. Catherine moved to South Africa where she was systematically abused by her father for two years before being rescued by her grandmother who took the toddler back home to Perth. However, life with her grandmother was also hard. She forbade other children from coming into the house and therefore most of Catherine's free time was spent alone, where she continued to go unloved and sink further into a morose existence. When Catherine's grandmother suffered a severe epileptic fit, she was deemed no longer fit to look after the young girl and Catherine was shipped off to another relative. This time Catherine moved in with her aunt and uncle in the Perth suburb of Lathlain.

Life for Catherine was extremely dull and she rarely smiled. Her upbringing was rather strict. Yet in a neighbour she found what she yearned for. When David Birnie came into her life she found a kindred spirit. The fast talking, intelligent David swept her off her feet and showed her the wild side of life and her own personality. Yet the relationship was short-lived as both teenagers were moved away by their families and soon lost contact.

David grew up as a scrawny boy; he was short and thin and often picked on at school. David left school at around fourteen and went to work as an apprentice jockey, a job perfect for his stature. He talked at length about his work with horses. He claimed that had he not been dismissed from the job due being suspected of stealing, he may never have gone on to commit the killing spree.[2]

In 1966, at the age of fifteen, Catherine and David met once again. This time David was wilder and drew Catherine deep into his world. He had quite an extensive juvenile criminal record for robbery and assault and an accomplice would suit him well. Catherine had also left school by this time and was working as a machinist in a window blind factory. But she was soon joining David in his criminal activities. By 1969, the 18-year-old couple found themselves in front of the magistrate in Perth Police Court several times, charged with breaking and entering and stealing. Both pleaded guilty to the charges and were remanded for sentencing. David received a prison term of nine months due to his previous extensive record for similar crimes. Catherine, who was pregnant with another man's child, was put on probation. The young lovers were not apart for long.

On 21 June 1970, David walked out of Karnet Gaol and found his way back to Catherine. Together, they committed a string of thefts that added another two and a half years to David's prison term. Catherine was sent to jail for six months and her newborn baby was taken from her by welfare authorities. After serving their prison terms, the couple went their separate ways again for a short time. David married and had a daughter. He settled down to family life. Believing she was rehabilitated and with the stipulation that she was not to see David Birnie, Catherine was released from prison and was granted custody of her child. She quickly found work as a live-in nanny for the respectable MacLaughlan family. Catherine fell pregnant to the son of her employers, Donald, and on her twenty-first birthday, 31 May 1972, the pair married. November saw the birth of 'little' Donny Jnr, and the couple seemed happy with their newfound family, a new experience for Catherine. However, the happy family would not last long. At the age of seven months, Donny was crushed by a friend's car and Catherine witnessed the accident.

Catherine and Donald made it through the terrible death together and had six more children. Donald was working as a council employee and though times could get a little tight, their family always had enough money to live on. However, after Donald injured his back he was no longer able to work and the couple, with their six children, were forced to live in a dilapidated government-provided house. The place was unkempt and the children ran wild most of the time. Catherine was exhausted and soon grew sick of life in poverty.

Around the same time, David appeared again on the scene and the two began an affair that would last two years, before Catherine finally rang her husband and told him she would not be returning. She left behind, in the Housing Commission house, her husband, her six children, her father and uncle. The couple was now destined to be together. They moved into a house in Willagee, Western Australia and Catherine changed her name by deed poll to Birnie. When questioned why the couple never married, David would explain that it 'just never came up'.[3] He believed that the relationship was always going to be volatile and by not being married it gave Catherine a way of escape should things become too difficult.[4] Nonetheless, the fire was now lit and David's sexual appetite was soon whetted. The couple would spend hours in bed having sex, often trying out new sexual positions or toys, between prison sentences for theft.

During one prison stint, David was reunited with his younger brother James; they were in fact cellmates at one time. James was in prison for the indecent assault of a 6-year-old girl. His defence had been that she had led him on. It was obvious that sexual deviancy ran in the Birnie family. According to James, David was heavily into kinky sex and had quite a huge pornographic collection. He wanted sex about six times a day, and would inject anaesthetic into his penis so he could last longer without ejaculating. When Catherine and David broke up for a short time in 1984, David forced James to submit to anal intercourse. In August 1986, James was allowed to have sex with Catherine as a twenty-first birthday present. The incestuous relationship would continue until David's final incarceration. David Birnie was a brilliant conversationalist. He was a knowledgeable man on many subjects, from the Australian Constitution to Chaos Theory and the building of the pyramids; his erudition amazed and inspired Catherine. He was able to talk her into anything he wanted. Soon, David wanted to rape and murder and Catherine was easily talked into assisting.[5]

Sex for the couple became boring and so they began talking about abduction and rape for kicks. Catherine said she would love to watch David penetrate another woman who was gagged and tied up. She told him how she wanted to lick his penis as it went in and out of another woman's vagina. The talk didn't last long before action took over. David decided it was time to act, and with Catherine's devotion he knew he would get his wish. The first victim was happened upon almost by accident. According to David,[6] on 6 October 1986, he was working at a car-wreckers when 22-year-old student Mary Neilson asked him about the purchase of some tyres for her car. There was an instant flash. David knew that the pretty young woman standing in front of him would be a perfect victim. Looking around to make sure his boss was out of earshot, he explained to Mary that he could do her a better deal. He said he had some new tyres at home. He gave Mary the address in Willagee and told her to come after 5 p.m. Later that evening, Mary arrived on the doorstep of the Birnies' home. Though still unsure if he could go through with it, David decided it was time to act. The pretty young student with long brown wavy hair accepted the offer to enter the house, and as she did, David seized her.

Mary was dragged to the bedroom where she was chained up and gagged to stop her screaming. David repeatedly raped the terrified young girl as Catherine stood and watched, encouraging her partner. Catherine and David then drove their frightened victim out to the Gleneagles National Park where David raped Mary again before grabbing a rope from the car and using a tree branch to garrotte the young woman. He then dug a shallow grave and threw the woman's body into the hole. Before covering the woman in dirt, he stabbed her in the chest to make sure she was dead.

Within two weeks, David Birnie was on the hunt again. The couple realised that having people come to the house was an easy way to entrap victims. So they advertised for their next victims in the local classifieds: 'Urgent. Looking for a lonely young person. Prefer female 18 to 24 years, share single bedroom flat'. It is unknown if anyone answered the advertisement, however no victims were accosted this way. The next victim was found hitchhiking alone along the Stirling Highway.

Susannah Candy was a young, free-spirited girl of only fifteen. She happily accepted the lift in a car by the friendly and seemingly harmless-looking couple. Susannah thought that, with a woman in the car, she would be safe. She was wrong. No sooner was Susannah in the car than she was tied up and driven back to the couple's house at knifepoint. David had been disappointed last time when they killed Mary so quickly. This time David knew he wanted to keep victim alive for longer. But he knew it was a risk. If someone had seen Susannah get into their car or enter their house, then they may be caught. To prevent this from happening, David forced Susannah to write reassuring letters to her parents, letting them she was okay. She was also made to ring them, reading a script written by Catherine.

Like Mary, Susannah was chained to the bed and raped and sodomised repeatedly by David over several days. Catherine also joined them in bed on occasions; she knew this would turn David on even more. Once David was finished with his sex slave he tried to manually strangle the fifteen-year-old. However, the young girl was too strong and fought to save her life. So, the couple drugged her with sleeping pills. When Susannah fell into a comatose state, David gave Catherine rope and told her to prove her love for him and kill the girl. Catherine willingly pulled the rope tight around Susannah's throat until she had stopped breathing. They took the body out to Gleneagles Forest again and buried her adjacent to the gravesite of Mary Neilson.

On 1 November 1986, 31-year old flight attendant Noelene Patterson became the Birnies' third victim. Noelene knew Catherine and David quite well. In fact, the couple had helped Noelene a few weeks earlier wallpaper a room in her house. Noelene had been having a bad day when she had run out of petrol. Standing by her car, angry at her silly mistake, she was relieved to see Catherine and David pull up beside her. But Noelene's relief soon turned to horror when a knife was held to her throat. The Birnies took their sex slave home, chained her to the bed, gagged her and raped her repeatedly. Catherine was concerned this time. She knew that David had always liked Noelene and Catherine was worried the woman may come between them. After several days of continual rape, David did not want to dispose of Noelene. He kept putting it off. Noelene was kept prisoner for three days before Catherine held a knife to her own throat and said that David had to choose between the two of them. David forced sleeping pills down the victim's throat and strangled the unconscious woman as Catherine watched. Then the body was taken to the forest to join the others. Only three days after Noelene's murder, another victim was abducted.

On 4 November 1986, Denise Brown was picked up by the couple as she waited at a bus stop near the Stirling Highway turnoff. For some unknown reason, she accepted the lift from the friendly strangers rather than wait for her bus. A knife was thrust to her throat as she got comfortable in the car. She was the Birnies' slave now. Denise, like the others, was taken to the couple's house at Willagee, chained to the bed and repeatedly raped for two days. Like Susannah she was made to call her parents to let them know she was okay. Catherine decided that time was up for the young woman and so Denise was bundled back into the car and take to Gnangara Pine Plantation the next afternoon. The couple drove into the plantation and while waiting for darkness, David raped Denise again.

Catherine held a torch for light as David plunged a knife into Denise's neck while he continued to rape her. Denise survived the knife's cuts. She was still alive and making terrible gurgling noises. Catherine could not stand the sound and so returned to the car to get a bigger knife. David plunged the knife into the woman's chest. Denise stopped moving and so the pair dug a shallow grave and put Denise into it. As the killer couple tossed the earth over the woman's body, Denise sat up in the grave and began struggling for air. David grabbed the shovel he had been using to the dig the hole and swung it at the girl's skull, but again Denise fought to right herself. David then bashed the young woman's head in with an axe.

Denise was finally dead. Catherine felt sick after the murder of Denise. She could no longer help David abduct girls. But David easily convinced Catherine that it would be better next time. Catherine conceded to David's plans, but she still felt that she could not go through with another murder like Denise's.

David did not give Catherine time to change her mind. He was now manic about murder and had such a lust for blood that the rampage had to continue.[7] The final victim was abducted only three days later. On 9 November 1986, David and Catherine abducted a seventeen-year-old young woman who was hitchhiking along Stirling Highway. She too was bound and gagged and driven back to the house. Inside the bedroom, the young woman was confined and subjected to a day of sex and violence.

During the time she was held prisoner she was also made to ring her family and tell them she was okay. David told the young woman that if she told them anything that she would be 'murdered like the others. During the ordeal, David and Catherine left their prisoner alone and untied while they made a drug deal in another room of the house. The captive took the opportunity to escape. She hid her bag and cigarettes under the bed before she left as proof she had been there. She was a smart woman and had kept her wits about her during her entire ordeal. Consequently, the woman ran from the house, covering her body with the little clothing that still hung from her arms. She stumbled to nearby Fremantle Shopping Centre, where police were called.

Once at the police station, the young woman told the interviewing officers of her ordeal at the hands of the sex-crazed couple. The girl directed the police back to the house and told them they would find her bag and cigarettes, proof of her stay. Police arrived at the house to find no one home. So, they lay in wait. Shortly afterwards, Catherine came home and was arrested. David was found at work as if nothing had happened and was also taken into custody.

Overnight, both Catherine and David were placed in separate rooms where they sat in silence. The police tried everything to make the couple talk to no avail. Police knew without their admissions they could only be charge with the abduction and rape of the young woman. Yet the police knew there were more victims and like David had told his captive, he had murdered them. Finally, in exhaustion one of the detectives said to David, 'It's getting dark, why don't you just show me where the bodies are, so we can dig them up'. David realised that the rampage of sex and violence was over. He would not be getting away with murder. He had known that this time would come.[8] He looked at the officers and said 'Okay, there is four of them'. Instantly the case took on huge momentum. With David's confession, Catherine also broke her silence and soon the couple, with a cavalcade of police cars, descended on Wanneroo Pine Plantation.

After some initial problems finding the burial grounds, David pointed to the graves of Mary Nielson and Susannah Candy and police crime scene technicians began the arduous task of digging up the victims. Catherine wanted to point out the next grave. With police watching, the hardened woman pointed to the grave of Noelene Patterson. With indignation for Noelene, a perceived threat to her love for David, Catherine spat on her grave. Denise Brown was also unearthed at another nearby plantation. On 12 November, the pair were charged with four counts of murder and one count of abduction and rape. No plea was entered.

At the hearing on 10 February 1987, Catherine and David pleaded guilty to all charges. According to David it was to save the families the tragedy of a trial in what he described in his confession as 'the most macabre and sadistic crime in the history of Australia'[9], a claim he continued to maintain until his death.[10] David was sentenced the same day. He was to be incarcerated for life, with the presiding judge Mr Justice Wallace saying, 'Each of these horrible crimes were premeditated, planned and carried out cruelly and relentlessly, over a comparatively short period …[David] should not be let out of prison, ever'.[11] David's sentence was termed 'never to be released', a proposal that is given to Australia's worse criminals.

A month later Catherine was sentenced to the same, however, she had a minimum term set and would eligible for parole in 2007. The judge said that Catherine lacked and remorse and 'each [murder] was premeditated, calculated and carried forward to its conclusion without mercy ...'[12] To date, she has been denied parole. In a letter to one of her children she tried to apologise, telling them that she was 'not proud of what has been said about me but I have to live with and the memories. As to why this happened I can only hope that the doctors can help me to find out'.[13]

Birnie also suffered a loss of his own. Catherine had begun her own parole proceedings and decided she stood a better chance if she severed all ties with David. After a number of unanswered letters, David realised that Catherine, after seventeen years in prison, had finally decided to end their relationship. The end of their relationship came as a bit of a shock to David, but he continued to wish Catherine well. There were no hard feelings and he knew that she had done it in the hope of a future out of prison. On 7 October, 2005, just a few hours after David was interviewed by the author of this book, he committed suicide.

At 4.30 a.m. on 7 October 2005, David Birnie was found hanging by a sheet in his cell in Casuarina Prison. He had been suffering quite severe depression at the time, and his health was failing, with numerous operations in the years preceding his death, his last comments were a line from the *Hitchhikers Guide to the*

Galaxy, 'Funny, how just when you think life can't possibly get any worse, it suddenly does'.[14] It was a small glimpse into the killer's train of thought. He was buried in an unmarked pauper's grave after his death as no one claimed his body.

Ivan Milat

On 19 September, 1992, a bushwalker hiking through the Belanglo State Forest in New South Wales stumbled across the remains of a young woman in a shallow grave. It was obvious that she had suffered multiple stab wounds in a frenzied attack. The discovery shocked the residents of nearby Berrima. The search was now on. Police identified the corpse as that of Joanne Lesley Walters from England, who went missing while backpacking along the Hume Highway with her friend, Caroline Clarke. So, what had happened to Caroline? It wasn't long until police knew the answer to that question. The following day police found the remains of Caroline. She was found only a few metres from where Joanne had met her brutal fate. She had been shot more than ten times through her head. The discovery of the two bodies would only scratch the surface of a crueller and more sinister plot of death and destruction.

Thirteen months after the discovery of Joanne and Caroline, police uncovered the bodies of Deborah Everist and James Gibson who were found in similar circumstances. Parts of the skeletal remains of Deborah were found in two shallow graves—she had been stabbed and her jaw and skull fractured. James had more serious blows with stab wounds shattering his bones. Then, one after the other, the remains of Simone Schmidl, Gabor Neugebauer and Anja Habschied were found, all in shallow graves and all with sickening injuries. The cowardly killer had stabbed Simone in the back a number of times. Six bullets shattered Gabor's skull and, if that wasn't enough, he was also strangled as if to finish him off. The most horrific injuries were those inflicted on Anja. Her head had been severed from her body in one bloody strike. The stabbing blows to her body were so fierce that she, like James, had chips knocked out of her bones with each strike.

The murders had caused such an outcry that a murderer had to be found, and fast.

While police kept searching the ghostly forest floor, the families of the dead backpackers sat waiting for the right lead to come along. Six months later it did; in the early hours of Sunday, 22 May, 1994, a man was arrested at his Eagle Vale home. He was to go down in the history books as Australia's worst serial killer. Ivan Milat was arrested on charges of armed robbery and possession of firearms. Though police refused to say whether they had a suspect for the 'Backpacker Murders', the media knew something was important about Ivan Milat. Within a few days, Ivan Milat was charged with the seven brutal murders and one attempted murder of a British backpacker known as 'A' or, as later revealed, Paul Onions.

Earlier in February, 1994, residents of Eagle Vale and the quiet street Cinnabar began to notice something rather peculiar. A plumber's van kept stopping at several street corners for no apparent reason, checking things out in the sleepy neighbourhood. As the van's appearance became more frequent, some residents rang the police to complain about the van 'patrolling' the streets of Eagle Vale. The residents around Cinnabar Street thought that perhaps someone was planning a robbery. The police assured worried residents that there was nothing to worry about as the van was 'one of theirs'. Soon a variety of cars were spotted acting suspiciously in the area. Usually they were white or blue Holden Commodores. Some residents even spotted a BMW motorcycle circling the same block. The plumber's van was usually seen near the large sporting complex beside my own home. The large car park on the hill gave the driver a superb view of the backyards of Eagle Vale. As the complaints and telephone calls to police increased, worried residents were told that they should not worry as it was part of a 'major surveillance and they should remain quiet about what they have seen.'

Then the climax to the nationwide manhunt broke at dawn on that fateful Sunday morning in May, 1994. A convoy of police cars and vans entered the still-sleeping suburban street and blocked off both ends of Cinnabar Street. Some residents who had seen the convoy of cars converging noticed the familiar plumber's van and BMW motorbike in the parade amid the fifty-odd cars. A white Tarago van screeched to a halt in front of the well-groomed pink brick home at number 22. From the van sprang five heavily armed State Protection Group police in black uniforms. The men bashed on the front door of the pink brick home, to no avail. Another police officer called the residents who were inside number 22. Again, the occupants did not leave the home. After ten minutes of telephone calls and officers knocking on the front door, finally a man appeared at the front door dressed in a checked blue shirt and jeans. He was dragged onto the dewy lawn and officers screamed 'get down, get down'. The man was forced to lie face down. Several officers aimed their guns at the man's head. Others screamed for him to put his hands above his head. Australia's most wanted killer had been arrested.

Simultaneously, one hundred heavily armed police swooped on two more properties in the Hill Top area belonging to Milat's brother, Walter. At one property, the search uncovered enough firearms to outfit a small army, two backpacks, several pieces of clothing, carpet and a leather bag. Also taken were thousands of bullet casings found on the two properties as well as anything else the crime scene technicians thought may have been evidence. All the items were bagged and loaded into the waiting four-wheel drive and table-top truck. Many of the seized items were found in a locked underground storage room. According to neighbours, the room had been built less than three years ago, just after the first Belanglo murder had occurred.

Another fifty police officers were at the other Hill Top property. They searched methodically through two old caravans that were hidden in dense bushland on the man's property. Also searched were two garden sheds and two cars. Carpet, clothing and firearms were taken as evidence for further testing. At the end of the Hill Top searches, Walter Milat was arrested for the possession of prohibited weapons. There were swoops made on several other homes that day. The Guilford house of Milat's mother was searched, as was another home at Mittagong. At Bargo another property was searched while nearly two hundred police searched a property at Buxton. Richard Milat was arrested at Moss Vale when police swooped on yet another property. At Wombeyan Caves, a remote property was searched, as were a further three properties in Ulladulla and Queensland. All were properties owned by Milat family members. Police searched the properties methodically, combing through rugged bushland. They dug up acres of bushland surrounding the numerous properties, taking photos and notes at every step. Several cars were also meticulously examined for evidence.

Ivan Robert Marko Milat was arrested on charges of the possession of prohibited weapons and appeared in Campbelltown Court on Tuesday, 31 May, 1994. The charges covered weapons and a silencer found at his home in Eagle Vale. He was also charged with not taking responsible precautions to ensure the safekeeping of the weapons in his possession. Furthermore, at his brother's Hill Top property, Ivan was apparently responsible for the possession of more prohibited weapons including a paint-ball gun, twelve-gauge shotgun with a nine-slot magazine, a crossbow, two Chinese barrels with receivers (one SKS and one SKK) and a replica .44 calibre six-chamber percussion revolver. Milat also owned a 4.10 double-barrel shotgun, a Raikal double-barrelled shotgun, two .177 calibre Dianna air rifles, one .22 calibre Ruger rifle, a .22 calibre Anschutz rifle, a 30/30 calibre rifle, a Chinese SLR and several containers of ammunition for the weapons. For the weapons listed, Milat was charged with carelessness in the safekeeping of weaponry. Walter Francis Milat was charged with not holding a licence for the firearms found at the property.

After a week in custody, Milat was finally charged with the seven murders. According to the police brief, Milat murdered:

- Deborah Phyllis Everist and James Harold Gibson on or about 30 December, 1989.

- Simone Loretta Schmidl on or about 20 January, 1991.

- Gabor Kurt Neugebauer and Anja Susanne Habschied on or about 26 December, 1991.

- Joanne Lesley Walters and Caroline Jane Clarke on or about 18 April, 1992.

- Milat was also charged with the attempted murder of Paul Onions, who was known only as 'A' during the trial, on 25 January, 1990.

At the hearing, as the charges against him were read out, Ivan Milat sat impassively. His appearance in court was far removed from the pictures that the public had seen only days before. Gone were the jeans and flannelette shirt, in their place was a light blue pin-striped suit. His drooping moustache and unshaven face was now clean-shaven. His face showed no expression as Crown Prosecutor Ian Lloyd, QC read out the grisly account of the fate of the seven backpackers and the Englishman. Milat's solicitor, John Marsden, described the charges as based on 'circumstantial innuendo' and that his client 'denies these allegations.' Though Milat denied the charges through his lawyer to the media, he did not enter a formal plea and so the hearing was adjourned until 28 June, 1994. When Milat re-entered the courtroom on Tuesday, 28 June, he declared that he no longer wanted John Marsden, the lawyer he had used for more than 20 years, to represent him. Milat claimed that the whole affair was a police frame-up and he likened himself to Lindy Chamberlain. He argued that there was nothing a solicitor could do for him while he was in jail, as there was 'not one iota of proof'. Milat decided that he would represent himself for the entirety of the trial and continued in outbursts during the hearing, accusing police of dragging out the case. He said they were making up more allegations as time went on.

However, the court did not agree, saying that more evidence kept coming to light, with the most recent being an army surplus water bottle. The bottle had been seized in one of the raids and it was obvious that a name had been unsuccessfully scrubbed off it. Using infrared photography, police analysts were able to enhance the name. The name 'Simi', a nickname used by murdered backpacker Simone Schmidl, proved that the bottle had been owned by one of the victims.

Additionally, other evidence seized at the homes of Richard, William and Walter Milat allegedly given to them by their brother Ivan 'to mind for him' were to further implicate Milat as the Backpacker Killer. Among the property seized was a backpack similar to the one owned by Simone Schmidl as well as a mat and sleeping bag similar to that owned by Caroline Clarke. Magistrate Kevin Flack informed Milat that though he may not want the legal representation of John Marsden, he should reconsider representing himself due to the severity of the charges.

Milat next appeared in court a week later, a little more subdued than in his previous court appearance, and despite his claims that he would represent himself, Andrew Boe a young Brisbane solicitor, appeared beside him. Milat's new solicitor began by making it clear to the packed courtroom that his client was innocent and that even though the media had provided not only photographs of Milat, but stories of past charges, his client would not be disadvantaged. The charges Andrew Boe was referring to were the charges of the rape of a backpacker in 1971. The magistrate made it clear that there was no conviction in that case but furthered the statement by saying that bail would not be granted this time, as Milat had fled the country after the allegations of rape had occurred in the 1970s. No application was made for bail and none was granted.

An odd point of the trial then occurred. A man with long hair pulled back in a bandana stood up in the public gallery. He called out: 'Can I speak for Ivan; can I say something?'. The man was told to sit down as he had 'no part in proceedings'. The hearing was adjourned at the request of Milat's lawyer, Boe. Boe was granted special leave to appear by Magistrate Peter Ashton, due to the fact that Boe was not a member of the NSW Bar. Obviously, Boe was linked to the Milat family in Queensland. Had Milat staged his previous court performance where he dramatically sacked John Marsden so he could get Boe, his brother's solicitor?

Outside the courthouse, Milat's sister told the media that what her brother had been charged with was obviously not something to be proud of. The hearing reopened at Central Local Court in Sydney on Friday, 5 August, 1994. Mr Boe brought up allegations that the prosecution was withholding evidence crucial to the defence. Milat's lawyer told the court that evidence had come to hand and that the prosecution was in possession of a statement by

Milat's brother, Alex. Andrew Boe told the court that Alex Milat had approached the police with the evidence that he and a friend had seen a man—not Ivan— with the two British backpackers in Belanglo Forest at Easter 1992. Police claimed they had interviewed the other man but he could not corroborate Alex Milat's story.

The Crown deemed that Alex's statement was unreliable and so was not needed to be handed to the defence. It was an insult to the defence team, which claimed any possibility that someone else may have taken the girls was important, and should have been submitted as evidence. Mr Boe also failed in trying to have the lesser charges of firearm possession, and the attempted murder of Paul Onions, heard separately. Prosecutor Mr Lloyd told the court that all the charges should be heard together because the evidence of the charges were 'strikingly similar' to the evidence of the murders. The defence's request was denied.

While their brother was in jail, Richard and Walter Milat both pleaded guilty to the charges of the possession of prohibited firearms. Magistrate Peter Ashton convicted Richard on four charges—two for the possession of illegal firearms including a crossbow, one charge for the possession of a licence in the name of Paul Miller, and another charge for the possession of marijuana. Walter was sentenced to seven counts of possession of illegal firearms as well as the possession of marijuana in a supply amount.

Counsel for the two men was John Marsden, the same lawyer who was sacked by Ivan Milat at the initial hearing. He claimed that the two men had been treated unfairly and would not have come under police suspicion if it were not for the charges brought against their brother Ivan. Marsden also came to the Milat brothers' defence, claiming that the cannabis found on their properties was for their own personal use and not for sale as the prosecution suggested. Marsden said in his statement that the men should be judged by whether their behaviour was legal, not on their obsession with guns. Marsden continued, saying: '[Richard] obviously likes guns, likes to play with them, and considers them items of pleasure when they [the brothers] go and shoot feral animals on his property at Wombeyan Caves... because we find that odd...I don't think we can judge them on that'. In applying for varied bail conditions (weekly parole, instead of incarceration) for Walter Milat, Marsden told the court that both men and the rest of the family had been under an enormous amount of stress since their arrest that fateful Sunday morning.

On 27 December, 1944, Ivan Robert Marko Milat was born to his Croatian-born father, Stephen, and his Australian-born mother, Margaret. He was the fourth child in an extremely large family of fourteen. The family nicknamed the young boy Mac, though none of them can actually remember where or when the name originated. The family lived in a small suburban three-bedroom yellow weatherboard house in Guilford. Out of the ten boys, most of them, including Ivan, went to Patrician Brothers High School in the south-western Sydney area of Liverpool. The younger members of the family attended the local schools in Guilford.

While at school, Ivan played football well but performed poorly academically, according to Ivan[15], at school if you did not perform to a high standard 'you would get your butt kicked for not pulling your weight.' School was a stoic environment, which obviously helped build the character of the boys. Most of the Milat boys did not stay at school for very long. Stephen worked seven days a week yet it still was not enough to feed the family of sixteen. The choice for the Milat boys was to either go out and get a job and help pay the bills and board or get out and fend for yourself, so Ivan left school at the age of fifteen. He went to work in roads and construction and had jobs all over Sydney.

According to Walter, Ivan's father was strict but fair. If any of the children got into strife, he would whack them to the ground. Ivan, like his brothers, got on well with his father. He was a devoted son who always paid his share of the board and kept the weatherboard house neat and tidy. Ivan also took special care of his younger brother David, who at a young age lost his arm and suffered irreparable brain damage in a car accident. He looked after his parents whenever he was home. Wally remembers how the other members of the family would get up late on a Sunday and just hang around, but Ivan Milat would get up early and mow the lawn for his father.

Ivan and some of his brothers enjoyed shooting and became familiar with many different firearms from a very early age. They remember knowing a lot of people who kept guns—it was a common thing in Ivan's life. On starting a job with the DMR (later known as the RTA) at the Central Asphalt at Granville, he also got his brother Wally a job there. His employers were so impressed by his work that he was made the leading hand. He worked on the construction gang for about fifteen years until all of the employees were retrenched. Due to his extensive experience, was quickly hired by Readymix, where he was still working at the time of his arrest.

Ivan met his future wife in the late seventies. They married and bought a house in the western suburb of Mount Druitt. They divorced during the early to mid-eighties and since the divorce Milat had a few relationships, though nothing serious. A few years before his arrest he met another lady who remained with him during the trial.

Milat was an impeccably neat person. Neighbours interviewed by the press could not believe what had happened. They described Ivan as someone who got on well with the children in Cinnabar Street, even letting them ride his mini-bike and go-kart. He often washed his car and attended to his perfectly manicured lawn.

Ivan's father, Stephen, who was twenty years his wife's senior died in 1983 at the age of eighty-one. The family had watched him suffer through bowel cancer which saw him undergo several operations. During his last operation Stephen contracted pneumonia, which led to his demise. Ivan looked after his mother as much as he could after his father's death, even buying her a new refrigerator when hers broke down.

Ivan Milat may seem to this point a rather devoted brother and son but there are a few tarnishes, which the public picked up on rather quickly. As mentioned, Milat was brought up on charges of raping a young backpacker in 1971. When released on bail, Milat fled to New Zealand to avoid being charged; he was rearrested in 1974 when he arrived back in Australia. Crown Prosecutor Lloyd agreed with the defence that the charges had been dropped, however the fact that he had jumped bail suggested guilt. Prior to the rape charge, Milat had criminal convictions for car theft.

On 29 December, 1989, Deborah Everist and James Gibson told friends they were going to hitchhike together along the Hume Highway to Albury on the NSW–Victorian border. Deborah was hesitant to go but decided to accompany James to an anti-logging rally. The pair was last seen leaving a backpacker hostel in Surry Hills on 30 December and, like the other five backpackers, they were to have their journey cut dramatically short. They were reported missing two weeks later on 15 January, 1990. Their disappearance sparked no immediate attention as many backpackers often lose their way for a while, or take exciting detours as they attempt to see the world, but soon their families began to fear the worst.

On 31 December, 1989, before the couple had even been missed, James' camera was found on the side of Galston Road, Galston Gorge, about 150 kilometres in the opposite direction of where the pair was meant to be travelling. Then, on 13 March, 1990, another fateful piece of evidence was discovered. James' backpack was found, again at Galston Gorge, only a kilometre from where his camera had been located three months earlier. The articles confirmed the worst fears for the two families.

On 25 January, 1990, Englishman Paul Onions had alighted from a train at Casula. Casula Station was a tiny, unmanned platform at the base of a steep hill. Many hitchhikers knew that it was the station to get out at because it was close to the start of the Hume Highway that would take them to Victoria and they could save the few dollars it cost for a train ticket.

Paul Onions' story was no different. His intention was to hitchhike from Sydney to Melbourne and the best place to get a lift was at the start of the Hume Highway. Paul climbed the steep hill from Casula Station and stopped at the little milk bar on the main road; the man stocked up on a few drinks needed for his trip south.

Paul was approached by a man who called himself Bill. At trial, Paul identified the man as looking like Ivan Milat and described the man's 'Merv Hughes' handlebar moustache. 'Bill' (Milat) offered Paul a lift and the man readily accepted. He got into the man's 4WD vehicle and they soon headed along the highway. The men made small talk and 'Bill' appeared to be a typical Aussie bloke talking about politics and all manner of things. As the car neared the turn-off to Belanglo State Forest, 'Bill' stopped the car, telling Paul that he wanted to get some cassette tapes from under the seat to help pass the time. Paul decided to use the opportunity to stretch his legs and probably saved his own life by doing so.

As he went to hop back in the car, the man called 'Bill' was holding a gun pointed straight at Paul. He said to the scared Englishman: 'This is a robbery...get back in the car' Paul was frozen to the spot. He could not move as he watched the man retrieve ropes from an old bag under the seat. Paul Onions realised what was about to happen and refused to be captured. He turned away from the car and began running away along the highway.

'Bill' also leapt out of the car and began waving the gun. He yelled at Paul, 'Stop or I'll shoot...get back in the car.' The man then aimed the gun at the hitchhiker and fired. Paul, in fear of his life, cleverly began running in a zig-zag motion to avoid being hit. He ran across the busy freeway with cars whizzing by. Eventually the man caught up to Paul and tackled him to the ground on the grassy median strip.

Paul fought for his life against his attacker and was able to flee once more. The frightened Englishman ran down the middle of the freeway and attempted to flag down a number of cars until one finally screeched to a halt. Paul Onions jumped into the sliding rear-door of Joanne Berry's van and screamed for her to drive away quickly. Frightened for the lives of her children in the backseat, Joanne did what she was told. Paul Onions stared out of the back window, watching the face of his attacker as the car sped away. Once away from immediate danger, Paul explained to the woman what had occurred and together they went to Bowral Police Station where a statement was taken. No action was taken on the report and the original record of Paul Onions' statement was eventually lost.

German backpacker Simone Schmidl, aged twenty, left Sydney on 20 January, 1991. She had intended to travel from Sydney to Melbourne where she was to meet her mother Erwinea. They planned to then rent a campervan and travel around Australia. Simone, like the other victims, disappeared somewhere along the Hume Highway. When Simone did not meet her mother in Melbourne after five days, Erwinea notified police. Simone's name was added to the list of backpackers who had disappeared.

Simone had backpacked around the world before. Her mother had begged her not to hitchhike along the highways, however Simone was young and didn't think any harm would come to her. After being missing for two weeks, a few news items appeared seeking information about the young woman's disappearance. 'Mother pleads for missing daughter' read one article. Another began with 'Fears for missing hitchhike girl'. Erwinea became frantic as time went on without word from her daughter. Eventually, Simone's mother returned home to Regensburg, near Munich, without her daughter.

Another German backpacker went missing around the same time as Simone. Carmen Verheyden was last seen at the Crossroads Hotel, near Liverpool, where the Hume Highway begins. The young woman had attempted to hitchhike to Westmead in Sydney's west where she was living at the time she disappeared. Carmen had attended a party in Minto and then gone on to the Crossroads Hotel for a couple of drinks with friends before leaving after midnight to hitch a ride home. According to some sources, the woman was likely murdered by someone she knew. Others suspected she was a victim of the Backpacker Killer. She remains missing. However, Simone's body was recovered as police searched the forest floor.

German backpackers, twenty-one-year-old Gabor Neugebauer and his girlfriend Anja Habschied, twenty, were Milat's next victims. The couple had been travelling around

Australia when Milat picked them up while they were hitchhiking the highway south from Sydney on 26 December, 1991. Other backpackers remembered seeing the young couple leaving the YMCA Hostel in Kings Cross the day after Christmas. The couple spoke of their plans to head through Melbourne and then across to Adelaide in South Australia before heading north to Darwin.

When the couple did not contact their parents in Germany after several weeks, they became concerned. Fearing the worst, their families flew to Australia and searched for their children. After several months they left to return home to their lives. It was as though their children had disappeared without a trace.

British backpackers, Caroline Clarke and Joanne Walters, left a Kings Cross hostel on 16 April, 1992. Like many other young people, they were going to see the world on a shoestring budget. They had planned to travel from Sydney along the Hume Highway to Victoria. They were seen several times along their travels, once getting into a truck at the Caltex service station at Bulli and again drinking at the Blue Boar Inn in Bowral. The women were unaware that they were only a few days away from their deaths. The women were last seen at Boxvale Walking Trail picnic area in the company of a man. When the two girls had not been in contact with their families in England for several days panic began to creep into the minds of their parents. Finally, after what probably seemed like an eternity to the Walters and Clarke families, Joanne and Caroline were reported missing on 27 May, 1992 and 5 June, 1992 respectively. The next time the young women were seen, they had been brutally murdered. The two British women were the last killed by the Backpacker Killer but they would be the first found.

On 19 September, 1992, two men who were on a map-reading exercise in dense bushland stumbled across the body of Joanne Walters in the north-west area of Belanglo State Forest, an area that the media would incorrectly call 'Executioner's Drop'.

The woman was wedged under a rock ledge, her body only partially covered by a thin layer of leaf matter. Joanne had been gagged with a cloth and two more pieces of her clothing covered her face. Her body had suffered multiple stab wounds in what could only be called a frenzied attack. The wounds covered the top half of both her front and back torso. Forensic evidence later revealed that Joanne had also been sexually assaulted. The following day, the body of Caroline Clarke was discovered in a shallow grave. Her remains were a mere thirty metres from where her friend was found brutally murdered. Caroline's body was beside a fallen log and was covered with leaf debris. Due to the layer of mulch, her body had decomposed faster than her travelling companion's body. However, like Joanne, Caroline's head had been covered before her death. This time the killer used a red sweatshirt to dehumanise his victim before killing her. The examination of Caroline's body showed that she had been shot ten times in the head. She had also been stabbed in the lower back, rendering her paralysed. Though it is unclear, evidence did suggest that Caroline may have also been sexually assaulted.

The shots had been fired through the red material that covered her head. Three shots entered the woman's head from the right-hand side towards the back of the skull. Two shots entered the left-hand side nearing the rear of her skull. Three bullets entered Caroline's head near the top of her spine, and two final shots were fired into the front of the woman's skull. From the ten gunshot wounds, five bullets were recovered from inside the woman's brain, two were found in the red jumper that covered her head and the three remaining bullets were located under her head on the forest's floor.

It was obvious that the woman had been shot dead, with excessive force, exactly where she had been found. Ballistics evidence proved that markings from some of the bullets indicated that a silencer had been used to prevent anyone in the area from hearing the murder. During the search on Milat's home, police found a home-made silencer in the garage.

The discovery of the English backpackers' bodies began a search that would not turn up anything more for over a year. Though a small piece of closure had come for the English families, police were still looking for at least five more backpackers who had gone missing over the years prior.

At 1.30pm on 5 October, 1993, a local man, fossicking along a lonely track with a metal detector in the Belanglo State Forest, stumbled onto a horrific find. The man had discovered what appeared to be a human skeleton. Unlike the bodies of Caroline and Joanne, these remains were completely uncovered. The killer had made no attempt to hide the victim. The man, not knowing what to do, grabbed the skull and drove to the nearest police station where he got the full attention of those on shift. With police in tow, the man returned to the forest to show them where he had made the discovery.

Police were worried that they had now found a third victim, and the words 'serial killer' began to echo through the ghostly pine forest. The police began a search of the immediate area around the victim, and assumed the body they had found may have been Anja Habschied, one of two missing German backpackers. Unbeknownst to police, only twenty-five metres from the body they were investigating lay an old fallen tree. The tree was actually an eerie headstone for a second shallow grave. A search around the first body was conducted and hours later, as the shadows crept along the forest floor, police discovered the second ghoulish grave. When the body was discovered to be a male, Police assumed they had found the missing German backpackers.

However, police were wrong. The bodies were actually those of James Gibson and Deborah Everist who had gone missing in 1989. This was verified by the estimated time since the death of the discovered bodies. Experts said that the bodies had been exposed to the elements for between three and five years, disqualifying the Germans as the victims seeing as they had last been seen only a year earlier. Three days after the bodies were found, they were positively identified through dental records as being James and Deborah. As their bodies had been reduced to bones, finding wounds and a cause of death proved difficult, though not out of the question. There was enough evidence to show that Deborah had suffered many strikes with a knife; slicing marks were found on her bones. Deborah had also been struck with something heavy that fractured her skull. Furthermore, the murderer had broken the young woman's jaw, probably as he punched her with force to ensure she stayed where she was while her attacker (or attackers) began a frenzied assault on her travelling companion, James, who had been tied up during her attack. A knotted pair of pantyhose found near James' body suggested that this was the logical scenario.

With James tied up, the murderer knew he was able to focus only on Deborah without being attacked or ambushed by James. This would also mean that there was no chance of escape for the two backpackers, meaning that again, the attacker would not be identified, leaving him free to kill repeatedly. There was no evidence to prove if Deborah's killer raped her. James' body, though very much decayed, showed evidence that he too was stabbed. It was clearly visible that James had suffered many strikes of his murderer's knife. A forensic examination later performed on James revealed he had been stabbed with such ferocity that the murderer had actually sliced some of his bones clean in half. There were also chip marks on his bones from other knife wounds. How the young pair died caused an outcry from the public. The two double murders were the work of a madman, and residents in the nearby towns of Berrima and Moss Vale demanded that police work harder to catch the person or persons who committed the horrible crimes. Police now felt the heat.

Though many of the townsfolk knew that the murders were the work of the same person, the police–though admitting the locality, types of murders and means of disposal were similar between the four murders, refused to admit that they were the work of a serial killer. The end of the worry had finally come for the families of James and Deborah who had waited nearly four years in anguish to find out the brutal fate of their children. Now they only hoped that police would find the bastard who had killed their children in such a horrific manner.

It was amazing that Deborah and James' skeletal remains were a mere six hundred metres east of the site where Joanne Walters and Caroline Clarke had been found, yet remained undiscovered for all of that time through several police searches.

Even though police had been looking for the killer for more than a year, they were no closer to finding the killer of Caroline and Joanne and the discovery of the bodies of Deborah and James did not make this task any easier.

By November, 1993, police could no longer deny that the murders were the work of a serial killer as they searched the forest floor for other missing backpackers. By now the families of Anja Habschied, Gabor Neugebauer and Simone Schmidl, among others, worried that their children would also turn up in the deadly forest. Police knew there had to be more bodies in the forest. The skeletal remains of Simone were recovered on 1 November, 1993.

The scene was only one and a half kilometres from where the remains of Deborah and James were discovered in early October. Simone was the fifth body found in a very small area. Police began to worry about how many more bodies would turn up before they had emptied Belanglo Forest of all its dark, morbid secrets. The sight that greeted police on that day was a haunting recurrence of the other four victims. Simone's body was lying beside a large fallen log. Like the others, she had been buried in a shallow grave with leaf mulch as a covering. Her body was covered in the horrific stab wounds that the killer had inflicted on the other victims. Her shirt was torn through with stab wounds. The time delay between her body being discovered and her death meant that most of the evidence that would have helped convict someone of the crimes had deteriorated.

Finally, three days after the discovery of Simone's body, the remains of Anja Habschied and Gabor Neugebauer were also recovered, taking the death toll to seven. Gabor had been shot six times in the head. Three shots had been fired into the left side of his skull, and a further three to the rear of his skull. Gabor had also been strangled. Inside the young man's mouth a piece of cloth was found. Another piece of material was found around his face, suggesting it had been tied as a gag. This time, there had been a struggle between the killer and his victim. Gabor had fought back and was shot while he attempted to protect Anja.

Yet Anja had also died, and her death was by far the worst. Her murder was a far cry from the wounds inflicted on the other backpacker victims. Anja's head had been severed from her body in one violent blow. It would have taken great force and a massive, sharp weapon to do such horrific damage in one strike. To date, the young woman's head has not been found and police believe an animal may have carried it away or the killer might have taken it as a souvenir and hidden it. The lower half of her body was naked and her clothes were nowhere to be found. However, due to the time lapse between her murder and the discovery of her body, there was not enough evidence to prove conclusively that a sexual assault had occurred.

Finally, after months of delays, the trial of Ivan Milat opened in Sydney in March, 1996. Media scrambled to cover every piece of evidence that was brought out in court. Photographs of the victims' shirts covered in stab wounds were flashed across every news broadcast. The case covered a mountain of evidence, each part just a piece in the puzzle.

As the case wound down to its dramatic conclusion, the defence team tried one last tactic. They asked the question that many of us had already asked. Was it possible that Ivan had not acted alone? Anyone who had studied the case was of the opinion that a second, and possibly even a third still walks free. Nonetheless, the jury, now down to eleven due to illness, provided the verdict everyone expected. Ivan Milat was found guilty of all seven murders as well as the attempted murder of Paul Onions. He was sentenced to life imprisonment with the recommendation that he never be released. Since his incarceration, Milat has gone on several hunger strikes to bring attention to his plight without success.

He has also been called to answer questions regarding the disappearances of Deborah Balken and Gillian Jamieson. During discussions I have had with the killer regarding the unsolved disappearances, he emphatically denied any involvement in the case, citing the fact that the man last seen with the women was a smoker and drinker. His wording suggested that though he may not be the killer he knows who it is. When pressed for further

information, Milat changed the subject.

Martin Bryant

I was studying for a criminology assignment with a group of friends many years ago when a news flash appeared on the television. The person on screen gave a grave description of a gunman in the convict ruins of Port Arthur in Tasmania. We had heard preliminary reports all day and decided to watch the news to see what exactly was going on. We were studying criminology and knew that what we were seeing was far worse than what we had been studying. We watched in horror, all of us writing notes on the preliminary reports of who the shooter was and the number of wounded and murdered tourists. We noted how the killer was shooting at police helicopters and ambulances as they attempted to recover the dead and injured. The news flashes continued into the night and the climax came the following morning at 8.30am when the Seascape Cottage, five kilometres north of Port Arthur, was razed by fire. The gunman fled the inferno and finally surrendered to police. He was on fire, his skin burning, and his clothes were gone but his wounds were nothing compared to the trauma, terror and destruction he had created over the previous thirty hours. Unnervingly, the killer appeared in court smiling and laughing as the murder charges were read. He was keen to know the number of murders to see if he had murdered more than any other. He had succeeded.

So, who was the man responsible for the carnage? With his long, blond, wavy hair, Martin Bryant looked like he would be more at home on a beach than in control of an AR-15 rifle, but as the layers were revealed, we found that Bryant was indeed a scary and dangerous young man.

Bryant had spent the evening before the massacre at Port Arthur having dinner with his mother and girlfriend. The next morning, he headed out for the day. He had many errands to attend to before the day's events could unfold. The first place he went to in his distinctive yellow Volvo was the Mid-Point Newsagents. He went inside and asked them if they sold cigarette lighters. When he was told they did, he returned to his car to get his wallet. He paid for the cigarette lighter and left the store without waiting for his change. From there he got back into his car and drove to the local supermarket where he purchased tomato sauce before heading to a petrol station where he bought a cup of coffee. It was an unlikely start for the day of a mass murder. He told the service station attendant that he was on his way to Roaring Beach to surf for the rest of the morning. Finishing his coffee, Bryant drove to another petrol station, where he purchased petrol, and again the man told the salesperson that he was heading to the beach for a surf. Was he trying to set up alibis for what was about to happen?

Instead of heading to the beach, Bryant headed towards the Seascape Guest House, a quaint bed-and-breakfast that he had tried to purchase several times before the massacre.[16] Sunday, 28 April, 1996, was a gloriously sunny day, after a miserable few weeks of rain and wind. Bryant walked up to the front door of the Seascape Guest House and knocked on the door. Seeing that it was Bryant, the couple David and Noelene Martin opened the door.

With a gun in his hand, he fired several shots above the heads of the frightened owners. Bryant had now started the mission he had set out on. He made the couple get down on the floor as he tied them up and gagged them. He was in total control of the situation. He then retrieved a knife from the bag and stabbed David Martin to death.[17] It was possible that he also murdered David's wife Noelene during this first attack. Leaving the Seascape, Bryant headed towards the historic Port Arthur Battlements.

Many tourists had already arrived at the historic ruins of the Port Arthur Penal Settlement. There were about 1500 people in the area enjoying the Anzac Day long weekend at the tourist attraction. At lunch time, the Broad Arrow Café did a brisk trade. The café was made out of the bricks convicts had made 150 years earlier. It had an outdoor eating area where people could sit and look out over the ruins as they enjoyed their lunch. Others would sit inside, looking out through the big glass doors. Broad Arrow was a popular place to visit whilst in Port Arthur and over the years many thousands of people had eaten at the café. Tragically, its last day of trade was the day that Martin Bryant came in for lunch. He entered the café, just after 1.00pm, and ordered his lunch. In his hand he held a Prince brand sports bag. At the time no-one seemed to take much notice of the twenty-eight-year-old. The staff member behind the counter said hello to Bryant, recognising him as someone who lived in the area. Bryant sat down and quickly ate his lunch. His heart was pumping, the pulse racing through the sides of his skull as he ate his food. He attempted to strike up a conversation with a woman sitting near him by saying: 'Great day, isn't it? Hey, there's not a lot of Japs out today. What do you think about that? There are a lot of WASPS, though, a lot of yuppies.'[18] The woman, not wanting to get into a racial debate with the odd young man, moved away from Bryant.

It was time for him to take the gun from the sports bag. Bryant reached down to the bag at his feet and took out the automatic rifle. He stood up and aimed the gun at the closest person. Two gunshots rang out.

The time was 1.27pm, and the first victims of the Port Arthur Massacre were dead. Malaysian couple, Moh Yee Ng and Sou Leng Chung had come to Australia to visit the beautiful countryside. Instead, they found themselves in the firing line of a madman. Bryant had shot Moh Yee in the neck[19] as he sat at the table closest to the killer. His companion Sou Leng had little time to react when she too was shot dead as Bryant aimed the rifle at her head and fired. Both remained in their seats, slumped over their café meals.

The killer did not randomly fire into the crowd. He took aim and shot each victim with purpose and intent. In the next fifteen seconds, a further ten victims were slain, and many others injured.[20]

Kate Scott was the third person to be killed at the Broad Arrow Café. The killer had fired a shot at her boyfriend, Mick Sargent. The bullet narrowly missed killing the man. Mick fell to the ground beside the café table from the force of the shot and luckily, survived. However, the fourth shot was more successful. Kate Elizabeth Scott was shot in the head and instantly fell like a dropped rag doll. Mick attempted to shield Kate from further injury but it was too late, Kate was already dead. Mick was too scared to look up in fear that the killer was aiming the gun at his head but he soon realised that the killer had turned his attention elsewhere.

Seeing the carnage unfold in front of him, Anthony Nightingale stood up. He had been seated directly in front of Bryant and called out in horror, 'No, not here.' They were the man's final words. Bryant aimed the rifle at Anthony and fired. A bullet penetrated the man's throat and he was killed instantly.

Walter Bennett was trying to flee the carnage with friends, Ray and Kevin Sharp, and their wives when the gunman turned the gun towards them. They all instinctively covered their wives. Walter and Ray were killed with a single bullet. Bryant aimed the rifle at Walter, and fired. The bullet hit him in the throat and continued further, killing Ray with a hit to his skull. Kevin was struck in the arm by a bullet that ricocheted, hitting three other people. A second bullet struck Kevin in the head, killing him as their wives cowered beside them.[21]

Bryant shot with precision. He did not waste bullets by shooting indiscriminately. His movements were purposeful and deliberate as he took aim and shot each victim with relish. By now, though only ten seconds had elapsed from the first gunshots, people who were still alive began searching for a way out of the café. Bryant stood in front of one door and fired at those cowering near him.

Andrew Mills and Tony Kistan attempted to flee with their friends and loved ones. Tony pushed his wife out the front doors of the café, as Bryant took aim. Mrs Kistan was the only person to escape through the front doors. The woman ran screaming from the horrific scene, too scared to look back. In those fleeting moments, she hoped Tony and Andrew Mills were behind her. However, the men had been killed. Again, single gunshots had stopped the men.

Bryant was losing his skill as the adrenalin surged through his body. The next two shots only wounded victims. Graham Colyer and Mary Howard were both hit by bullets and sustained horrific injuries. Luckily, the two were able to live to tell of their horrific injuries. Mervyn and Mary Elizabeth Howard were not so lucky. The couple, along with many other diners, had tried to flee through the kitchen. As people scrambled to hide in cupboards or behind doors, Mervyn was shot in the head then Mary Elizabeth was also shot dead.

Sarah Loughton was the next one in Bryant's firing line. As Sarah's mother tried to shield her from the gunfire, Bryant aimed the gun at Sarah and fired, killing her with a single gunshot to the head. Next, Bryant wounded Robert Elliot with a gunshot to the head before heading to the rear of the café.

Winifred Aplin had been cemented in fear to her seat when the gunfire began, and soon after Bryant murdered Sarah Loughton, he turned the gun towards Winifred and fired another shot. The bullet killed the mother of four instantly. In total, the entire carnage had lasted only fifteen seconds and twelve people lay dead in the café, with many others wounded from gunshots and shrapnel wounds.

Nicole Burgess was serving in the souvenir shop when she heard the gunfire start in the café next door. The sound had been deafening but she did not know what she was hearing. The sound was more like someone hitting a cardboard box rather than what she thought gunfire would sound like. She hid behind the counter with her cousin Elizabeth as Bryant came towards them. The man aimed the rifle at Nicole as she tried to hide. He fired a single shot, killing her.

Elizabeth Howard had also been serving in the souvenir shop with her cousin Nicole when the gunfire started. After killing

Nicole, Bryant took aim and killed Elizabeth. The man was splattered with the blood of his victims and his shoes were soaked through.

Leslie Lever stood in shock as he watched the murderous campaign. In the past twenty seconds, more than a dozen people had been killed. Many customers from the café had tried to flee through the souvenir shop and were now being pursued. The man was gunned down as the killer walked past him. Bryant turned again towards the café and fired a further shot, wounding another victim, Peter Crosswell.

Jason Winter was the next to die at the hands of the madman. The twenty-eight-year-old had been crouching under a table with his wife and baby son. The baby cried, terrified and confused by what he saw. Jason tried to console the baby when Bryant took aim. The man was killed instantly by a gunshot to the head. Bryant then turned his attention back to the souvenir shop where several customers had attempted to escape but found themselves up against a locked door.

Ronald Jary, along with Peter Nash and Pauline Masters, tried to flee through a door in the souvenir shop, only to find it locked. The trio looked into the eyes of the gunman as he took aim and fired a single shot into each of their heads. The victims had no way of escape and could do little against the man with the rifle.

Sixty-six-year-old Ron Neander and his sixty-seven-year-old wife Gwen were on their first holiday from South Australia in many years. The elderly couple was separated in the shocking carnage as people tried to avoid certain death. As Ron called out to Gwen, the woman came face to face with Bryant. The man aimed the gun at her and fired. When Ron found Gwen, she was lying in a pool of her own blood. Ron went into shock. Around him were twenty dead people and dozens had been injured, yet the killer had only used twenty-nine bullets. He then changed the magazine in his rifle and prepared for the next part of the carnage. What seemed like hours was only ninety seconds.[22]

As the carnage continued, Broad Arrow worker Brigid Cook had run out of the back door, screaming for people to get away. The woman saved countless people from the massacre that had played out inside the café yet she herself did not believe what was happening. Brigid also ran towards the bus car park where people were milling around, waiting to head to their next destination.

She was screaming hysterically that they should seek cover as the killer followed her towards the tourist transport buses. The woman's bravery probably saved dozens of lives as Bryant gunned her down, shooting her in the legs.

As people hid behind the buses, a witness took a video of Bryant walking purposefully around the buses looking for people to kill—eerie and terrifying footage. Coach driver Royce Thompson heard Brigid screaming and came around the side of one of the buses to find himself staring down the barrel of Bryant's rifle. The man tried to flee as the gunman fired. The bullet struck the man in the back. Though horrifically injured, the man rolled under a parked bus to stop the killer firing any further shots. Though he survived the initial gunshot, Royce later died in hospital from his injuries. Wendy Scurr made the first telephone call to police about what was happening at Port Arthur. The time was 1.32pm, only five minutes after Bryant fired the first shot.[23]

Fifty-three-year-old Neville Quin and Janette, his fifty-year-old wife, had come to Port Arthur on a bus trip. They had been standing near the buses when they heard Brigid Cook screaming for everyone to hide as Bryant came upon them. Bryant took aim and shot Jan in the back as she took cover in the car park. Bryant then looked at Neville, who was frozen in shock. Bryant raised his gun as Neville ran onto the bus. Bryant shot at him, however the bullet missed its target. It was the only bullet to miss.

Bryant hissed at the man: 'No-one gets away from me.' He chased Neville and shot him in the neck. Neville survived his injuries. Bryant decided to leave the area so he jumped into his yellow Volvo that he had parked near the exit to the historic ruins. However, the man then changed his mind and continued to shoot at people scrambling to safety. He noticed that Jan Quinn was still alive and was attempting to crawl along the ground. The killer walked up to the woman and fired another shot into her head, ensuring she was dead.

Elva Gaylard had watched in horror as the killer murdered Jan Quinn. She was even more fearful when she could no longer hear or see the killer. Little did she know, but Bryant had come up behind her. Elva turned to see Bryant raise the gun to her chest and fire. She fell back with a mortal wound to her chest and arm. She would later die in hospital as doctors fought to save her life.

While on the Port Arthur peninsula, Bryant had killed twenty-two people in a matter of minutes. However, the killer hadn't finished yet. Bryant, now back in his car, headed towards the front gates of the historical tourist attraction where he continued the carnage. Nanette Mikac and her two daughters, six-year-old Alannah and three-year-old Madeline had heard the gunfire and were fleeing the scene when Martin Bryant drove up beside them. Thinking the man was going to offer them a lift to safety, Nanette turned to Alannah and said: 'We're safe now, pumpkin'[24], as she held their hands and walked towards Bryant's car. Someone further down screamed at Nanette to run, trying to warn her that she was heading towards the killer. Bryant laughed and demanded that Nannette get down on her knees. Instinctively, Nanette pulled her two young daughters close to her and begged Bryant to spare them.

'Please don't hurt my babies,' she pleaded as Bryant aimed the gun at the woman's head and fired a single shot. Madeline, still in her mother's arms was shot in the arm and then in the chest. Alannah, having witnessed her mother's and sister's murders fled towards a tree, where Bryant gave chase. He fired two shots at the girl but missed. Alannah, terrified and sobbing, tried to shelter behind the tree, but Bryant was soon upon her. The man put the muzzle of the gun to the little girl's neck and fired. She was dead.

People tried to flee, telling people coming into the site to also leave as quickly as they could. People hid along tracks and behind bushes in an attempt to escape the gunman's fire. Tourists entering the tollgates abandoned their cars, however when Bryant arrived at the tollbooth in his own car, now unarmed, he began to argue with Robert Salzmann, whose car, along with many other abandoned cars were inadvertently blocking the man's escape route. The man, unaware of what had occurred at Port Arthur, kept at the heated exchange with Bryant until the killer reached into his car and grabbed another gun. He took aim and killed Robert with a single shot. The killer then pointed the gun at his wife Helene and pulled the trigger.

Russell Pollard had seen the exchange between Robert Salzmann and Bryant from his BMW that was parked in the queue of cars leading into Port Arthur. The man rushed from his car when Bryant shot Robert. However, Russell was also killed with a shot to the chest and the gunman then dragged Mary Nixon from the BMW's passenger seat and shot her dead. The killer then got into Russell's BMW and headed towards a nearby petrol station.

Near the petrol station, Bryant pulled the BMW over beside Glenn Pears' little white Corolla. He tried to pull Glenn's girlfriend Zoe from the car, threatening her with his gun. Glenn got out of the car and ran at Bryant as he attempted to protect Zoe from the gunman. Bryant pointed the gun at Glenn and forced him into the boot of the BMW. He then returned to the Corolla where he aimed the gun at Zoe and shot her dead. The killer drove off in the BMW with Glenn still inside the boot. Bryant drove to the Seascape Guest House, passing several cars. He continued to fire shots at passers-by, injuring several more people. Once at the cottage, Bryant took Glenn out of the boot of the car and tethered him to a railing inside the guesthouse. He then doused the car in petrol and set it on fire.

By now, most of the emergency services had been alerted to the massacre at Port Arthur and arrived, with police guards attempting to rescue the injured and the dying. What they saw was a war zone. Bodies lay piled up in the Broad Arrow Café, people nursed their dead loved ones, the floors and walls were covered in blood and people with horrific injuries of their own tried to help others. Many people did not talk about what they saw, they just knew they had to try to help. What had occurred was beyond anyone's comprehension. The tourist attraction's first aid officers tried to help with the little equipment they had — they would never have been prepared for such a mass of casualties. People used napkins and paper towels to stem the blood flow of those horrifically injured in the gunfire.

By now there weren't many tears. People were in shock and a quietness had settled over the area as loved ones held each other in the hope that the killer had gone or had been killed. There were many heroes that day who, despite their own injuries, still comforted the dead and dying. Families clung to each other, haunted by the unimaginable, terrorised beyond their worst nightmares.

At the Seascape the horror was still continuing. With the BMW on fire on the front lawn of the guesthouse, police believed it to be a beacon, showing them where to find the world's worst mass murderer. Inside the house, the phone had rung. A news reporter had tried to find out what was going on by calling the local businesses. She called the Seascape and Bryant answered the phone. She was relieved to finally get someone to answer. She asked him if he was aware of what had been happening at Port Arthur. Bryant, introducing himself as Jamie, said that he had lots of fun at Port Arthur, giggling hysterically as he did. The reporter knew instantly that she was speaking with the killer. He told her not to call back or he would kill his final victim.

The woman called police immediately. Officers were already on the scene, taking cover in the water run-off ditch at the front of the house. The man inside the guest house was firing at them. The stand-off had begun. The time was now 3.00pm, a mere two hours since the carnage began.[25]

At 9.00pm, police negotiators arrived on the scene in an attempt to talk 'Jamie' into giving himself up peacefully. The man inside the house demanded that police bring him a helicopter. He told them that to show good faith he would release one of his victims, Glenn Pears. The stand-off continued into the night with the killer maintaining telephone contact with the officers outside. The police tried to keep the man talking as much as they could.

When asked if he knew anything about the events at Port Arthur, Bryant was keen to find out how many he had killed. The police negotiator told Bryant that there were many injuries. There was silence before Bryant asked: 'They weren't killed?'[26] He seemed disappointed that there was a possibility his victims had survived.

Police tried to get close to the house but were told to get back by the killer. The situation got even worse. The cordless phone he was using inside the house went flat so no more communication was possible. Hours of silence followed, only to be broken by occasional gunfire from inside the house.

The killer knew he was cornered. At daybreak, police noticed smoke and fire inside the guesthouse. It was time to get any survivors out, though police believed that the killer was alone. They believed he had already murdered everyone inside the house. The fire raged out of control, quickly reaching his cache of weapons and exploding. Police rushed inside the house where they found the bodies of Glenn Pears and David and Noelene Martin. Bryant had shot Glenn Pears during the overnight stand-off. The killer fled the burning guesthouse, his clothes and flesh on fire. The flames on the man's body were extinguished and he was arrested. The killer was rushed to hospital for the treatment of his burns. Questioning would have to wait.

Later that evening in Royal Hobart Hospital, Detective Inspector John Warren interviewed Bryant for the first time. Bryant was sedated due to the burns he had sustained in the Seascape fire, yet he told the police officer that he was not responsible for the massacre as he had been surfing all day. Det Insp Warren noted down what the killer said before formally charging him with the murder of Kate Scott, one of the first victims at the Broad Arrow Café. The other charges were added shortly after, once the man was deemed mentally competent to stand trial.

At trial, the giggling blond-haired man was to answer thirty-five charges of murder, twenty charges of attempted murder, three charges of grievous bodily harm and eight charges of inflictions of wounds. He was also charged with four counts of aggravated assault, one count of unlawfully setting fire to property (Glenn

Pears' vehicle) and one charge of arson for the setting of fire to the Seascape Guest House. When the charges were read out in the court, the man covered his mouth as he giggled. His demeanour incensed the murder victims' families who had attended court to see the world's worst mass murderer.

At first, Bryant pleaded not guilty to all charges, claiming again that he had been surfing on the day of the murders. Yet many locals were able to identify him as the killer. The trial began in November, 1996, and the main focus of the case was Bryant's intellectual disabilities. According to the experts at trial, the man's IQ was borderline intellectually disabled. The families and victims were concerned that the man was going to walk free from the charges. Then, in a turn of events, Bryant changed his plea. He pleaded guilty to all charges, giggling as he did so. The judge passed sentence on 22 November, 1996. Bryant was given thirty-five life terms. Justice Cox told the young man that he should not ever be eligible for parole. For the remaining charges, the man was sentenced to a further twenty-one-years.

Bryant remains in protective custody in prison. The cache of weapons he had amassed was nothing short of shocking. Following the massacre, each state and territory of Australia toughened its gun laws in an attempt to prevent such a tragedy from ever happening again.

Ted Bundy

According to Ted Bundy, he was raised in what he called a "healthy home."[27] He felt safe and secure in the life he had with those he believed to be his parents. Unlike many murderers there was no religious mania, no sexual, physical or psychological abuse. He was shown love and encouragement, the family he knew remained settled most of his early life. Unlike cases such as serial killer Edmund Kemper who was locked in a cellar by his religiously zealous mother and later shipped off to grandparents whom he would kill when he was still a teenager, Ted Bundy's early childhood showed very little clues to the monster he would become. Yet even until the very end, he was able to find people who adored him. Even the trial judge Justice Edward Cowart, when passing the death sentence, showed admiration for the prolific serial killer saying, "Take care of yourself, young man. I say that to you sincerely; take care of yourself, please. It is an utter tragedy for this court to see such a total waste of humanity as I've experienced in this courtroom. You're a bright young man. You'd have made a good lawyer, and I would have loved to have you practice in front of me, but you went another way, partner. Take care of yourself. I don't feel any animosity toward you. I want you to know that. Once again, take care of yourself."

Ted Bundy was born Theodore Robert Cowell on November 24, 1947, unbeknownst to him during his childhood, he was the illegitimately son of Eleanor "Louise" Cowell. On Bundy's birth certificate Lloyd Marshall was named as his father, Eleanor also mentioned that another man, Jack Worthington as a possible candidate, however details have since surfaced that claim that his grandfather – Louise's father – could be the real father of Bundy.[28]

To avoid any scandal and to hide the truth for Ted, Louise moved in with her parents and Ted was brought up believing that he was their son. To him, his biological mother was known as his older sister Louise. To most, the situation was certainly not the perfectly healthy home that Bundy referred to in one of his last interviews before his execution, but he was referring to the fact that his family, though unconventional for a small child, was absent of sexual or physical abuse.

In 1951 Louise moved to another relative's place with Ted and a year later she met and married an army cook called John Bundy. Ted took Bundy's name though at the time he still did not know that Louise was his real mother. Bundy conceded that his early life was quite normal, he was raised in what he described as "a wonderful loving home where he was the focus of his parents' lives."[29]

He was often quick to turn any sort of blame for his killing ways away from his family and instead blamed external forces that turned him into one of the world's most prolific killers. As a boy of twelve, about to embrace puberty, Bundy discovered soft core pornography on magazine stands at local supermarkets, news agencies or even discarded in rubbish bins that lined the streets on garbage collection days. Yet quickly Bundy discovered that the semi-clothed women of the softer pornographic magazines he stole no longer fuelled his sexual fantasies. He sought out more explicit images. He went in search for harder pornography periodicals and detective magazines that combined violence with sexually explicit stories and images. He would search through rubbish bins and dumps, looking for discarded material that suited his taste for violent pornography.

In an interview in prison, he mused, "Sex and violence brings about behaviour that is too terrible to describe, I'm not blaming porn, it did not cause me to go out and do those terrible things, the issue is how this type of literature contributed, moulded and shaped my violent behaviour. In the beginning it fuels the thought processes that crystallises as a separate entity"[30] After his capture, Bundy was quick to separate the killer 'entity' from the rest of his personality.

At the same time as his sexual deviance commenced to simmer to the surface, Bundy learned that he was an illegitimate baby, but was not told of his true parentage. He threw himself into his studies, doing well at school and becoming popular, psychologists later described him as "intelligent, high achievement-oriented, had the acumen necessary for a political career"[31] a direction in life that he felt he could achieve had it not been for his other 'entity'. At school Bundy always felt a little out of place, yearning to be like the wealthier students of his high school. To try and achieve what the others had, and he was denied, he was suspected of committing several robberies to try and attain those things that his family could not afford. He was never caught nor charged with any offences.

On completion of high school where he graduated in 1965 he was accepted to the University of Washington, where he commenced studying for a degree in psychology, a weapon he would use during his murderous campaign to gain the trust of the women he abducted, and play with psychologists who tried to study him in prison. He claimed that his stealing became more prolific.

Between 1969 and 1972 Bundy sent applications to several law schools and became actively involved in politics for the first time. He carried out volunteer work at a crisis clinic in Washington before commencing in a job with King County Law and Justice Planning Office in Washington State tracking habitual criminals. During the same period, he found out that his older sister was his real mother, and his mother and father were really his grandparents. The news forced Bundy to close down part of his life and instead returned to his studies with vigour. It was one of the first moments where he learned to use disassociation, a feature people display when they are faced with uncomfortable feelings or emotions.[32] Bundy returned to Washington University and graduated. In September 1973 he accepted a position of entry in law at University of Puget Sound in Tacoma.

He again commenced seeing Stephanie Brooks, a young woman he had previously dated, but had broken up with when he had become belligerent. However, once she had seen the drive and success return to his life, they again started dating sporadically.

On January 4, 1974, Bundy brutally attacked his first victim. Eighteen-year-old student Joni Lenz was found unconscious and bleeding in her apartment bedroom the following morning. Bundy had broken into the woman's room the previous night and raped her. He had taken a rod torn from the bed head and savagely rammed into her vagina causing horrific internal injuries, he had also beaten the woman around the head. Joni was taken to hospital where she remained in a coma for several months. Joni survived the attack but was left with brain damage.

He broke up with his girlfriend, Stephanie purely to cause her the grief that she had caused him when she broke up with him the first time. He was angry and found a way to react to those emotions, coupled with the violent fantasies he had been having since puberty. He began raping and murdering young women who looked like his girlfriend.

On the night of January 31 1974, twenty-one-year-old Lynda Healy was beaten and abducted by Bundy from her basement level room at Washington State. Her room showed signs of the struggle and her bed was covered in blood, where Bundy had cut her throat after raping and sodomising her. Missing was the top sheet from her bed. Bundy had used it to bundle up his victim and remove her from her room. She was missing for two months before police took the case seriously, having first believed that she had suffered a bad nose bleed and gone to hospital.

Bundy, now having murdered his first victim, commenced on a savage killing spree that would last four years, though he was arrested several times, he would subsequently escape and continue to kill. Initially, he ensured that he remained in control, being careful to hide his victims so it would take months to find them, by which time, most forensic evidence was lost to the elements.

On February 8, 1974 20-year-old Carol Valenzuela disappeared in Vancouver. Her body was found later in October with the remains of another female who was never identified. Her murder and that of the unidentified victim found with her has been attributed to Bundy but she may have also been a victim of Warren Leslie Forest, another serial killer operating in the same region at the time.[33]

On March 12, 1974 another college student disappeared. Nineteen-year-old Donna Manson left her dorm room around seven in the evening to walk to a jazz concert on campus, along the route she was charmed by Bundy who possibly offered to walk with her or give her a lift to the concert in the drizzling rain that had begun to fall, either way Bundy was able to take the young Evergreen State student. Donna wasn't reported missing for six days because of her habit of travelling with little notice. She was never seen alive again.

Like Donna, eighteen-year-old Susan Rancourt disappeared as she walked across the campus of the college she attended. On the evening of April 17, 1974 Susan had made plans to join a friend to see a German film at Central Washington State College but she never arrived. She was last seen leaving a meeting with one of her advisors after nine that evening. It was the one and only time that Susan had gone outside at night alone, having heard about the previous abductions, the risk cost her her life.

On May 6, 1974 Bundy abducted another victim. Twenty year old Roberta Parks decided to walk to another dorm hall to have coffee with friends. She never arrived. Along her travels she had met with Bundy. Bundy had pretended to be handicapped by a broken arm. He dropped his books near the young woman who offered to pick them up for him. He convinced her to carry them to his car where he struck her over the head and abducted her.

Twenty-two year old Brenda Ball was the next to disappear. She was last seen at Flame Tavern in Burien on June 1, 1974. She had told friends she was going to find a ride to Sun Lakes, toward closing time she asked one of the musicians at the Tavern but he was unable to help her. She was last seen talking to Bundy in the parking lot. Like he had used with previous victims, he had arm in a sling. It took Brenda's friends nineteen days to realise she had not made it to Sun City and called police to report their friend missing.

On June 11, 1974 eighteen-year-old Georgann Hawkins was abducted from behind her sorority house, Kappa Alpha Theta in Seattle. Georgann had been to a party and left to say good night to her boyfriend and borrow some text books for a Spanish exam she was going home to cram for the next day. A friend of Georgann's saw her walking across campus and called out to her from a window. The two students chatted for a few minutes, they said goodnight and Georgann walked toward her dormitory. When she had not arrived home two hours later the alarm was raised. With the recent abductions in the area, the Seattle police acted immediately. A dorm mother had heard some screams but thought it was students mucking around outside and did not look to see what was going on. Had the dorm mother looked she may have seen Bundy using his handicap ruse on Georgann. Ted had asked Georgann for help carrying his briefcase to his car because of his fake cast, and she had obliged. He knocked her unconscious, stuffed her into the car and sped away. In the car, Bundy later recalled that Georgann had regained consciousness and in her confused state had she thought he'd been sent to help her with her Spanish exam. He knocked her out again, then pulled over near Lake Sammamish where he strangled her before raping her.

Bundy was becoming an expert at killing, so far, he had gotten away with at least eight murders. None of the bodies had been found and police were no closer to finding the person responsible for the abductions. He felt confident in his ability and he began escalating and next killed two women on the same day.

Janice Ott was the first one abducted by Bundy on July 14, 1974. Janice was feeling solemn, she was missing her husband who had stayed on at his practice in Riverside. She left a note for her roommate saying she was going to go for a bike ride around the park at Lake Sammamish. Later witnesses told police that they had seen a girl matching Janice's description talking to a friendly looking man who had a broken arm. It was the last time she was seen alive. Ted abducted her in front of everyone at the park without raising any suspicion. He took her into the woods where she was raped and murdered, like the other victims before her. Yet Bundy was not done. The abduction of Janice had happened so quickly and easily, that he went back and abducted another victim.

Nineteen-year-old Denise Naslund was having a picnic with friends on the Lake Sammamish that day as well. While the others fell asleep in the summer sun, Denise wandered off to the bathrooms, where she was spotted by Bundy. Like Janice before her, Bundy asked her for help to get something from his car, pointing again to his broken arm. She was happy to oblige and walked with him to his car. There she was forced inside and driven away to Bundy's dump site. She was bashed over the head and then raped.

With the murders playing on his mind, his 'normal' life was quickly losing its excitement and Bundy soon left his position with Emergency Services and instead looked again to study. By 30 August 1974 he was a student at University of Utah College of Law.

A week after Bundy commence his Law degree, bones were found scattered along a four kilometre stretch near Lake Sammamish State Park. The body parts were from the remains of Georgann Hawkins, Janice Ott and Denise Naslund.

The discovery of the bodies did little to damper the drive of Bundy, however he knew that he had to find a new dumping ground for his subsequent victims. On October 2, 1974 he abducted sixteen-year-old Nancy Wilcox in Holladay, he raped and sodomised her before killing her. Her body was never recovered.

On October 18, 1974 another young woman fell victim to Ted Bundy's charm. The Midvale Police Chief's daughter, seventeen-year-old Melissa Smith was abducted by Bundy between collecting some clothes from home and walking to a girlfriend's home. Nine days later on October 27, the bludgeoned and strangled remains of

Melissa were found in Summit Park. Like the other victims, she had been raped and sodomised before her murder. Her skull had been fractured by an instrument similar to a crowbar.

On October 31, seventeen-year-old Laura Aime left a Halloween party and went for a wander to a nearby park where she was abducted by Bundy. Her body was later found on a river bank in the Wasatch Mountains on November 27, 1974 Her naked body had been beaten beyond recognition. Like Melissa Smith, she had been sexually assaulted.

A little over a week later, on November 8, nineteen-year-old Carol DaRonch survived an abduction attempt. At a Waldens Bookstore she was approached by Bundy posing as a police officer, he had now changed his ruse from the handicapped man to a person in authority. He asked if she'd parked near Sears, and she had said yes. He asked for her license number and she gave it to him. Bundy then told Carol that someone had tried to break into her car, and she needed to go with him to check if anything was missing from her car. She trustingly followed him quietly out of the building, but felt a sudden apprehension as they headed out into the rainy night. Like the others before her, she had trusted Bundy quickly, at trial she described him as "polite...well educated."[34]

She asked him for some ID after realising that she had been a little too trusting and he responded by laughing at her, as he attempted to make her feel at ease for her stupid error and showed her a fake identification badge. The pair reached Carol's car and she saw that nothing was missing. He then told her that they had apprehended a suspect and asked her to go with him to the station in his VW Beetle to see if she knew the suspect. Carol felt that something wasn't right and then noticed an aroma of alcohol on the man's breath. Alarm bells sounded and she grew more aware of the situation she was in as they walked to his VW. She reluctantly got into the car after he gave her another convincing lie about being undercover. When he told her to put on her seatbelt, she said no, and was ready to jump, but he'd already driven off. She realized he was heading away from the local police station.

Suddenly he stopped the car and attempted to handcuff her, but in the struggle, connected both cuffs to the same wrist. As they struggled, he pulled out a small gun and threatened her with it but she opened the car door and fell out. As she got up Bundy attacked her with a crowbar that he had hidden under the driver's seat. He grabbed her and threw her up against the car. However, the diminutive Carol broke free from Bundy's grasp and ran wildly onto the road where an elderly couple came upon her and took the terrified girl to the police station.

After failing to abduct Carol, Bundy went looking for another victim that same evening. Seventeen-year-old Debby Kent had offered to pick up her brother while her parents stayed behind at her school's drama night. Later, another parent told police he had arrived late at the play and saw a light-coloured VW bug racing away from the school. A quick search by police discovered a small handcuff key in the parking lot. The key fit the cuffs that Carol DaRonch was wearing when she arrived earlier at the police station. While police investigated the disappearances and the attempted abduction of Carol DaRonch, the body of Laura was found on Thanksgiving. Like the others she had been raped and beaten.

After murdering four young women in a little over a month, Bundy spent the period between Thanksgiving and the New Year without killing. The police had linked many of the disappearances and were searching for a local man in Utah. After the New Year Bundy headed to Aspen in Colorado for his next murder, where police were not looking for a mass murderer.

On January 12 1975 Caryn Campbell was on a ski trip in Aspen Colorado with her fiancé and his kids. After a minor squabble with her partner she stormed off and headed back to their room. When she did not return he went to their room to see if she was there. However, she had never made it to the hotel room and was never seen alive again. Bundy had grabbed the woman as she had walked to her room, possibly using the police – stolen car ruse once more.[35]

On February 18th, 1975 as the weather slowly began to warm, the naked and battered body of Caryn Campbell was found in a snow bank off Owl Creek Rd, close to the hotel where she had been holidaying with her fiancé and children. She had been raped before being murdered. Police were quick to compare the injuries that Caryn had sustained with the injuries inflicted upon Melissa Smith and Laura Aime. Investigators noted, "You couldn't look at those photographs and autopsy slides and read those reports without noticing gross similarities." Bundy's signature was obvious. He had beaten all of his victims in a frenzied attack and had raped and sodomised them either before or after their deaths. The victims were all young women with similar features and were of good moral standing. None of them were taking freely, they had all been taken against their will. Unlike many killers who chose prostitutes or victims from low socio-economic backgrounds, Bundy chose those women who would be missed and who represented the type of woman he wanted to be with. There was even a resemblance to his former girlfriend and some of the victims, proving that the murders, though sexual in nature had a retaliatory element as well.

On March 1, 1975 the skull of twenty-two-year-old Brenda Ball was found in a thick wooded area on Taylor Mountain. Brenda had been missing since June 1974. The police began a search of the area and soon more gruesome discoveries were made. Parts of the skeletons of Lynda Healy, Susan Rancourt, Donna Manson and Roberta Parks were also found. The skull of Lynda Healy was fractured from the brutal beating she had suffered. Susan Rancourt's decapitated skull was also severely fractured.

The discovery of some of his victims did little to slow down Bundy in his killing spree. On March 15, 1975 twenty-six-year-old Julie Cunningham disappeared while on her way to a nearby tavern in Vail Colorado. Her body was never recovered.

On April 6, 1975 Denise Oliverson, twenty-five decided to go for a bike ride to visit her parents in Grand Junction after having an argument with her husband. When she didn't return that evening he assumed she had decided to stay the night at her parents. However, she had never made it to her parents' home. Along the trip she had been abducted by Bundy. Her body remains undiscovered. Nine days later on April 15, eighteen-year-old Melanie Cooley disappeared after walking off from school. Road workers discovered her body on April 23, 1975 at Nederland. She had been bludgeoned to death with a crowbar like many of the others. Her hands had been tied behind her back and a pillowcase was tied tightly around her neck.

Month after month, Bundy continued to abduct women, bludgeon and rape them before dumping their bodies. On May 6, 1975 Lynette Culver was abducted from her school playground, followed by Susan Curtis from a university campus on June 28, twenty-four-year-old Shelly Robertson was taken from Golden on July 1, 1975 and Nancy Bird was abducted on July 4 in Layton. The killing spree was causing Bundy to start acting irrational and take risks. As he searched for another victim on August 18, 1975, Bundy, stoned at the time was arrested in Salt Lake City for evading a police officer. He had seen the police vehicle following him but knowing that he had marijuana in the car and chosen to keep driving. The mounting killings were taking their toll. Bundy said of his arrest, "I really didn't know what was on my mind or what I wanted to do. I was a little bit fucked up."[36] When the officer searched the car, he found handcuffs, a crowbar, a ski mask, and pantyhose. Bundy was arrested for having implements for breaking and entering.

While on remand Bundy murdered another young woman. Debbie Smith was abducted and murdered in February 1976.

When the police officer told others about Bundy, his car and the handcuffs, one of the investigating officers quickly saw a link between Bundy and the man witnesses had seen with several of the murdered women. Carol DaRonch was brought in to see if she could identify Bundy as her would-be abductor. Carol DaRonch identified him as her attacker and he was placed under arrest. On March 1, 1976, after a trial in which Bundy represented himself he was convicted of the kidnapping charge of Carol DaRonch in Utah.

While in prison Bundy was charged with murder of Caryn Campbell, however he Bundy escaped from Pitkin County Courthouse lock-up in Aspen on June 6, 1977. On June 16 a very dishevelled Bundy was recaptured but again jail cells were unable to hold the killer and on December 31, 1977 Bundy escaped from jail in Glenwood Springs, Colorado and travelled through Denver, Chicago and Michigan.

By January 7, 1978 Bundy arrived in Tallahassee, Florida and rented a room in student boarding house. It had been two years since his last killing. He told the landlady he was a student and he spent his time roaming the nearby campuses looking for victims. His urge to kill surfaced again and the blood lust had reached a boiling point.

The Chi Omega sorority house at Florida State University was pretty quiet on the evening of January 15, 1978. But little did the female students know but a killer was stalking them, Bundy later would recall that having been in prison he had been unable to fulfil his need to kill, therefore once he had escaped, the vicious attack that was to occur at the Chi Omega sorority house was a manifestation of his need to harm.[37]

Sorority house member, twenty-one-year-old Karen Chandler had gone to bed around midnight, twenty-year old Lisa Levy had gone to bed around 11pm, twenty-year-old Kathy Kleiner went to bed around midnight and Margaret Bowman went to bed around 2.30 after talking to a girlfriend about a blind date she had had that evening. Cheryl Thomas returned home around 1:30 am. She had turned on the TV, made something to eat and fed her new kitten. Her friend Debbie who lived in the next room arrived home and shouted teasingly through the wall for her to turn down the TV.

At 4am Debbie woke to a strange hammering sound. She slept on a mattress on the floor and so she had felt the whole house vibrate from the thumps. She shook her roommate awake and they listened in fear until there was silence. Scared, they sat in the dark and listened. The two women heard Cheryl moaning from the next room so Debbie called Cheryl's room. The girls had a signal to always answer the phone regardless - just to make sure they were all always safe. When Cheryl didn't pick up the phone Debbie called out that she was going to call the police. As they were speaking to the police, they heard a great thunderous crash from Cheryl's apartment, as if someone was running and crashing through the kitchen. Debbie and her roommate were shocked to see a dozen police cars at their house within four minutes of their call.

As the sorority sisters headed down the hallway to the dorm-mother's room Karen staggered out into the hall from her room. Blood was streaming down her face, she had been savagely beaten. After seeing Karen, the housemother decided to begin checking the other rooms. Kathy was sitting on her bed; her head was in her hands and the blood ran down her arms from the wounds she had suffered. Her jaw was broken in three places. Lisa Levy had been beaten savagely, her right nipple had been almost bitten off, her left collarbone was broken, and she had been strangled. A hairspray bottle had been jammed into her vagina and there was a double bite mark on her left buttock, which would later help identify Ted Bundy. Paramedics tried to save her but she was pronounced dead at hospital. Twenty-one-year-old Margaret Bowman was found lying on her stomach across her bed. She had been beaten across the head with a crowbar which shattered her skull instantly. A stocking had been pulled tightly around her throat. She did not survive the attack.

Cheryl was the last of the women attacked by Bundy. She was found lying diagonally across her bed, barely conscious, whimpering and writhing in pain. Her face was turning purple with bruises, it was swollen and she had several serious head wounds. She suffered the worst injuries on that night but somehow survived the attack. Her skull was fractured in five places, causing permanent hearing loss in her left ear. Her left shoulder was dislocated, her jaw was broken, and her cranial nerve was so damaged that she would never have normal equilibrium. She would remain in the hospital for a month. If the girls hadn't shouted out about calling the police, Bundy would have killed Cheryl Thomas.

Bundy fled the scene into the night before police arrived, but only by minutes. In his wake he left the fullest extent of his brutal homicidal signature.

Less than a month later Bundy struck again, killing his youngest victim. Twelve-year-old Kimberly Leach disappeared on February 9, 1978. Kimberley had left class to go and find her wallet that she had left somewhere in the playground. She was seen by a friend talking to Bundy, it was the last time she was seen alive.

Though Ted Bundy was being sought all over America for the Chi Omega murders, and the string of other murders he had left in his wake, it would again be a traffic stop that brought the killer to justice. Bundy was arrest by a traffic officer in Pensacola, Florida on February 15, 1978 for driving a stolen car.

On April 12, 1978 after eight weeks of intense searching, the decomposed remains of Kimberley Leach were found hidden in a pigsty. She had been raped before being murdered.

Though Bundy attempted many different lines of defence during his trial he was sentenced to death plus 196 years for the murders of the students at Chi Omega House on July 13, 1979. Bundy was also sentenced to death by electrocution for the murder of Kimberley Leach on Feb. 9, 1980. During the courtroom trial, Bundy married serial killer groupie Carol Boone in a brief ceremony. On January 17, 1989, Florida Governor Bob Martinez signs Bundy's fourth death warrant. Bundy began to reveal information about more murders than those he has been sentenced, admitting to the murders of many of his suspected victims. The confessions were an attempt by Bundy to stave off the looming execution date. Often speaking about himself in the third person he gave many details of victims that had not been found, hoping the bargaining chips would work. It was too little too late and on

January 25 1989 Ted Bundy took his final seat in the arms of Old Sparky at Starke Prison Florida.

When confronted with the question of why. Why he had murdered so many young women, Ted Bundy chuckled to himself and asked, "is there really enough time to explain it all."[38] Reflectively, he explained that he could see how certain feelings that he was experiencing over his lifetime developed to a point that he commenced acting out on those destructive fantasies.[39]

The Wests

Claiming that deviant behaviour is 'what normal families do' is how sexual abuse and violence are often justified by family members. Warping a young child's understanding of what is normal can be achieved early in their life. Though not all child sexual abuse victims go on to become offenders themselves, almost one-third of them do. When two victims of child sexual abuse marry, the risk of their perpetuating such abuse is exponentially increased, such as in the case of Fred and Rose West, the serial-killing couple, both of whom were victims of childhood sexual abuse at the hands of their own parents.

Frederick Walter Stephen West was born in 1941 in Much Marcle, England, to Walter and Daisy West. Fred was the apple of his mother's eye, while his father, a stern man known for physically punishing his children, terrified Fred as a child. Living in a tiny English hamlet, the family often sharing one large bed, Fred was sexually abused by his mother and witnessed his father sexually abusing his sisters and other local girls. After his incestuous start to life, a sexual awakening occurred in the young boy, which saw him become extremely aggressive with the local girls. He spent his teenage years coercing young girls to have sex with him, often giving them promise rings if they allowed him to bed them.[40]

Following a motorcycle accident in November 1958, which left him in a coma for eight days, a metal plate was inserted in his head to hold his smashed skull together as it healed. He also broke his arm and one of his legs, resulting in a permanent limp. Following the accident, the usually carefree, though sexually aggressive young man was more morose, with an unpredictable temper, flying into sudden rages and striking out at those around him. Like his father, his violent streak was coupled with a voracious sexual appetite. It wasn't long before his behaviour would get him in to trouble.

In 1960, West suffered another brain injury following an attempt to have sex with a local girl. His victim had pushed him from a fire escape at a local youth club, causing him to fall and lose consciousness. It was also around this time that West was arrested for impregnating his 13-year-old sister.[41] At his trial for incestuous sexual assault, his sister refused to testify against him, leaving the police with little choice but to free him without a conviction. His father kicked him out of the house for bringing attention to the secret sexual deviance of the family, telling him never to return. West spent the next eighteen months travelling the countryside working odd jobs on construction sites.

In August 1962, the 20-year-old Fred met his future wife, 16-year-old pregnant runaway Catherine 'Rena' Bernadette Costello. Rena told Fred that she had escaped a home for wayward girls where she had been sent following a brush with the law. Before meeting Fred, she had worked as a prostitute and stripper, and was also a convicted thief. The young couple were instantly attracted and became lovers, but before the couple could further their relationship, Rena abruptly returned to Scotland.

Fred went home and begged his parents to forgive him for the assault of his 13-year-old sister. They relented and let him return to live with them. When Rena returned to March Marcle three month later, however, now heavily pregnant with her first child, Fred convinced his parents that he was the father of the baby and Rena moved into the West's tiny home. During their numerous arguments, Fred routinely beat Rena; the couple also fought with Fred's parents, who did not like their son's choice of partner.

Against his parents' wishes, Fred secretly married Rena on 17 November 1962, in a registry office in Ledbury, after which they moved to Scotland together. On 22 March of the following year, Rena gave birth to a daughter, Charmaine. While she was in hospital with her baby, Fred was at home, having sex with one of Rena's sisters.[42] He showed little interest in the baby, which wasn't his, preferring to spend his time bedding various local women.

Following the birth, Rena returned to her job as a stripper at a local club. There, Fred met Charmaine's Pakistani father, who according to Fred was also Rena's pimp. The man threatened West, telling him he was no longer allowed to have sex with his own wife. In lieu of Rena, he supplied Fred with many other girls for sex.

But Rena was already pregnant with West's baby. She tried to abort the unwanted pregnancy, without success, and in 1964 Anne-Marie West was born. Anne-Marie, like her older half-sister, would be subjected to a lifetime of sexual torture and abuse at the hands of her father, a plaything whom West repeatedly raped over the decades to come.

Following the birth of Anna Marie, West met 16-year-old Anna McFall, another teenage prostitute, who quickly fell under his spell. Anna moved into the home that West shared with Rena and worked as a nanny for the two babies. Fred was working as an ice-cream truck driver to support his wife, nanny and children, yet tragedy struck when he reversed the truck over a four-year-old boy, killing him. Though the death was an accident, Fred packed up his belongings and, along with his lover Anna McFall and the children, returned home to Much Marcle, leaving his wife behind. He put the two girls into government care while he found a job in a slaughterhouse, honing the dissecting skills he later used on many of his victims.

By the time Rena attempted to win back her husband, she found that Anna McFall had taken on the full-time role of 'wife' to Fred and mother to the children, a domestic situation that made Rena furious. She stormed into the local constabulary, where she spoke to a young officer, Constable Hazel Savage, who recorded Rena's complaint that she believed that Fred was molesting their children, demanding that they be removed from his care. It was one of the first encounters Constable Savage would have with the West family. She began investigating the claims, but Rena soon withdrew her complaint. Nonetheless, the police now knew that the family were an unconventional unit, requiring, at the very least, cursory monitoring. Savage would later be instrumental in uncovering the horrors that occurred in West's home at 25 Cromwell Street.

In 1967, Anna, now pregnant with West's child, demanded that he divorce his wife and marry her. Yet Fred had no desire to yield to her demands. Instead he moved Anna into another caravan whenever Rena visited. The arrangement was less than appealing to Anna, who complained to her mother in regular letters about the treatment she received at Fred's hand. West would often rape and beat her, and tried out many sadomasochistic sexual tortures on the young woman, which would feature heavily in the later murders.

Finally, in August 1967, Anna McFall disappeared while eight months pregnant with Fred's child. According to Fred's later confession, he stabbed her through the heart. Yet when her body was finally unearthed a quarter of a century later, it bore the hallmarks of a fatal torture session. Her hands were tied together behind her back and her body was clothed only in a light blue cardigan. Whether it was consensual or not will never be known.

Nonetheless, the pregnant woman was most certainly murdered by Fred, who then dismembered her body, removing several of her fingers and toes as well as the full-term foetus from her womb.

After her murder, he disposed of the woman by burying her in the green fields of Much Marcle. The specific place, Fingerpost Field, was land he had worked as a boy, alongside his abusive father. From his home he could look out over the field and see where he had buried Anna. He later confessed to his father that he had killed his young girlfriend; West and his father shared many dark secrets over the years, including their sexual interference with the West sisters and other local girls. When Fred told his father about Anna's murder, Walter replied, 'I'm not going to turn you in or nothing. If you can live with, I'll say nothing. Leave it.'[43] The body remained hidden until 1994.

Another young girl disappeared a few months later, in January 1968. Mary Bastholm, 15, disappeared while waiting for a bus in Gloucester. Though Fred never fully confessed to her murder, [44] it is likely that she was murdered by West and buried somewhere near the body of Anna McFall.

In February 1968, Fred's mother Daisy had a heart attack in February 1968 and subsequently died. It hit Fred hard. He became more morose than ever, beating his wife and two children excessively and molesting the little girls more frequently. The year was significant for another reason as well – 1968 was the year he first met Rosemary Letts, the young woman who would help shape the man into an even more terrible monster.

Rosemary Pauline Letts was born in November 1953 in Devon, England, the fifth child of Bill and Daisy Letts. Bill was a sadistic schizophrenic and her mother Daisy was undergoing shock therapy for depression when she fell pregnant with the girl they would call 'Dozy Rosey'.[45] Daisy Lett's depression was related to the violence she suffered at the hands of her husband, who would also strike out at the children, with a ferocity that was only matched by his own incestuous sexual appetite. Rosemary was known to rock herself so violently that she could fall into a catatonic state. This sort of unusual behaviour might have been the result of her conception during her mother's shock treatment, or a result of the violent abuse she suffered later.

Like Fred West, Rosemary failed at school and left with only the fundamentals of reading and writing. As her older sisters left home, Rosemary's father turned all of his sexually perverted attentions on his young daughter. In turn, the young girl learned to win favour with her father through her own sexual promiscuity, and consequently escaped the beatings her siblings suffered. She also inherited her father's violent and aggressive temper, beating her younger siblings or local children when the mood took her.

Finally, after years of abuse, Daisy Letts escaped the violent home, taking her daughter and two young sons with her. Yet the move did nothing to prevent Rosemary's sexually deviant behaviour. By the age of 14, she had seduced her younger brother, grooming him just as her father had done to her.

Following an affair with a man twice her age, Daisy moved again, this time leaving the teenage Rosemary behind to fend for herself. She moved back to live with her father, where she took on the roles of both daughter and lover. During this time, she was sexually assaulted by a man who grabbed her from a bus stop while she waiting for a lift home. The man dragged her into a park and savagely raped her. Some suspect her attacker might have been none other than her future husband Frederick West[46], but the attack was never reported and Rosemary continued her life as her father's sexual plaything. Then in summer 1968, Fred and Rosemary's lives officially collided. While working in a local bakery one day in February 1968, West looked up to see Rosemary walk through the store's door. The pair were instantly attracted to one another and began a sexual relationship almost immediately. Their sexually deviant partnership would prove fatal for the young women of Gloucester.

In the early 1970s, Fred took a job driving a van through the country. He would often pick up young hitchhikers, whom he would rape and torture before letting them go. Rosemary, pregnant at home with Fred's baby, would babysit his two young daughters, often spending her days beating and whipping them.

In October 1970, Rose gave birth to the couple's first child, Heather. In June 1971, Rose murdered Charmaine West, Fred's step-daughter. According to Fred's confession, his partner lost her temper with the young child. Rose, still a child herself, was the primary carer of Charmaine, Anna Marie and Heather while Fred was in prison for robbery offences. Fred's confession stated that Rose struck out at the defiant child, who refused to heed to her demands. The child was buried under the kitchen of the home the couple had rented in 25 Midland Road, Gloucester, possibly after Fred's release from prison. Charmaine's body had been cut up prior to the haphazard burial. When it was later unearthed, she was missing her fingers and kneecaps.

In August 1971, Fred decided it was time to get rid of Rena, to prevent her questioning Charmaine's disappearance. He got his wife highly intoxicated and drove her to Much Marcle, where he had buried Anna McFall. According to his confession, he made love to her twice before the pair got into a fight. Then he claimed to have killed her by smashing her into the iron gate that fenced the lush green paddocks from the roadway. He dismembered Anna's body and buried her in a shallow grave. Regardless of whether Rose played any part in the murder, she was aware that her lover had murdered his wife, and this secret almost certainly cemented their deviant relationship.

Suspecting how far she would go, Fred pushed the boundaries with his promiscuous partner. He began advertising her sexual services in magazines, with photographs of Rose prominently featured in the articles. Fred allowed Rose to use their own bedroom to service her clients, many of them West Indian, as long as he was able to watch through a peephole in the wall. Fred often would have rough or kinky sexual intercourse with Rose following her client sessions. Fred also video-recorded the sexual exploits of Rose and her clients. He believed he could use the tapes not only spice up his own sexual fantasies, but possibly to blackmail clients who had families and wives of their own.

The pair, bound by sex and murder, married in January 1972 at a Gloucester Registry Office. At the time, Rose was three months pregnant with Mae. After the birth of Mae in June of that year[47], Fred moved his family into their final home, 25 Cromwell Street in Gloucester. In 1994, the house where most of their victims' bodies were buried would be dubbed 'the House of Horrors' by the press. Fred chose the home specifically for its cellar. He had plans to convert it into a torture chamber where he would sexually abuse and torture his victims, including his children, over the next 20 years.

The first victim to be led to the cellar was his own daughter Anne-Marie. The eight-year-old was lured into the dark hole by her parents. She was tied up and gagged before being savagely raped by her father. She was told that what was happening would make her a better wife and mother later on.[48] The rape resulted in horrific injuries that required her to be away from school for several days while she recovered. Yet it was only the beginning of the abuse she would endure at the hands of those she would call her parents.

Caroline Owens was the next girl to be picked up by Fred. The 17-year-old accepted a job as a babysitter with the growing West family, but left the job by December 1972, fearing Fred's incessant sexual pursuit. A few months later, while hitchhiking home, she accepted a lift from Fred and Rose. Taken to their house, she was bound and gagged before being raped and beaten by the couple with a belt buckle.[49] After hours of abuse, the teenager was allowed to leave, as long as she promised not to report them. She did report the attack, but the pair were let off with a nominal fine, when Fred was able to convince the judge that Caroline had been a willing participant in their sexual games.[50]

Lynda Gough moved into the West house in April 1973. The 19-year-old had left a note for her parents saying she was going to move in with a nice couple to act as a babysitter to their children. Lynda began her time with the Wests as a willing accomplice in the sex games that Rose, pregnant for a third time, and Fred shared with her. Then one night Lynda found herself hanging by her ankles from the ceiling of the cellar's torture chamber. According to Fred's confessions, the young woman enjoyed the bondage game she was playing with the kinky couple, but soon their games turned deadly. 'In the hours, even days before her eventual death, Lynda Gough was reduced to nothing more than a slab of meat.'[51] Fred systematically sliced off pieces of the woman's body, in a torture method akin to the Chinese method of *ling chi*, which causes pain but does not kill quickly, victims instead dying slowly from blood loss, over several days. Before she was buried, Lynda's fingers, hands and forearms had been removed. When her body was later discovered under the garage of 25 Cromwell Street much later, 113 of her bones,[52] including her fingertips and kneecaps, were missing.

Four months after the murder of Lynda Gough, Rose gave birth to a son, Stephen. Yet having another baby in the house did little to stop the Wests' killing spree. Three months later, the couple chose their next victim, 15-year-old Carol Ann Cooper, who was last seen at a local pub. Fred picked up the young girl in November 1973. According to Fred, Rose was solely to blame for the young girl's murder in a 'kinky love sessions that went wrong'.[53] Carol was hung from a wooden beam in the cellar, Rose having placed a large elastic band around the girl's head and face to prevent her from calling out. Hanging helpless from the beam, she was beaten and abused for days, until she was finally murdered by the couple during one of their violent fantasy torture sessions, during which they severed the girl's head, possibly while she was still conscious.

By the time her mutilated corpse was buried, the couple had removed nearly 50 of her bones,[54] and many pounds of flesh.

Lucy Partington disappeared on 27 December 1973, having been offered a lift by a friendly-looking couple. They took her back to the Wests' home, where she was made to perform various sexual acts with Fred and Rose before she also was tortured, mutilated and murdered. Lucy's body was buried with a knife that had been used in her murder, as well as a large piece of rope that was still knotted around her throat. Her remains were missing 72 bones.[55]

Four months later, the West couple struck again. Therese Siegenthaler, a 21-year-old student, was picked up by Fred West while hitchhiking. Therese was tied up and taken down to the cellar, where she was tortured and mutilated, before her head was severed from her body and a further 37 bones removed. Her body was buried in a corner of the cellar. Fifteen-year-old Shirley Hubbard was the fifth girl to be murdered and buried at 25 Cromwell Street. On 14 November 1974, she ran away from the foster home where she lived and ended up at Cromwell Street. Once inside the cellar, Fred West engaged in bondage and covered the girl's face with tape, creating a mask that covered her entire face. He fed two tubes into her nostrils so she could breathe. Shirley was left there, trapped in the cellar for days, as the couple took turns beating and sexually assaulting her. Again, they sliced off pieces of her body until she finally died. According to Fred's confession, Shirley 'slipped off'[56] the hook where she had been hung upside-down.

Juanita Mott was the next to accept an offer to stay at Cromwell Street. The young girl had nowhere else to go and welcomed the offer from the couple. In April 1975, her lodging arrangement proved fatal. She was tied up with rope, and abused and tortured before her death. She looked to have been struck 'as if a ball-ended hammer had been hit against the skin'.[57] The young woman was decapitated and almost 90 of her bones were removed before she was buried in the cellar with the other bodies.

Two years later, the next victim was murdered. Shirley Robinson, 18, rented one of the upstairs bedrooms in the West home in Cromwell Street. The pretty green-eyed girl quickly became Fred's lover, often sharing a bed with both Fred and Rose. After Rose became pregnant to one of her Jamaican clients, Fred impregnated Shirley. Rose felt threatened by the younger and prettier woman who now took up most of Fred's attention, but in June 1977, Fred strangled Shirley as his wife slept. He buried the young woman and the unborn child he had cut from her womb in the back garden of Cromwell Street. Six months after the woman's murder, Rose gave birth to Tara.

In November 1978, a daughter, Louise was born to Fred and Rose. At the same time, Anne-Maire suffered an ectopic pregnancy that required the removal of one of her fallopian tubes. Fred was believed to be the father of her unborn baby.

The Wests lured another victim to her death in September 1979. Alison Chambers was brought to the couple's bedroom, where she was tied down, with another belt tied around her face to stop her screaming. They tortured her for the next several days before finally murdering her. The girl's partial remains, minus 96 bones, were buried near the back steps of the Cromwell Street home.

Meanwhile, Rosemary continued to have children. In June 1980, Barry West was born, followed two years later by Rosemary Junior, whose father was one of Rose's clients. A year after Rosemary Junior's birth came another mixed-race baby, Lucyanna, in July 1983. Anne-Marie had by then married and left the home, leaving Heather, one of the eldest children, to be sexually abused and harassed by their lecherous father. The family unit was beginning to break down. As the stories of the abuse suffered by the West children began to filter through the neighbourhood, it was not long before police attention was focused on Cromwell Street. By the time police searched the family home, however, it was too late for Heather. On 19 June 1987, she was killed, the final known victim of Fred and Rose West. Most observers of this case believe that no more murders occurred, though both Fred and Rose continued to threaten the other children with being buried in the garden like their sister.

Five years after Heather's disappearance, in August 1992, police executed a search warrant on 25 Cromwell Street. Complaints had been raised through child services, claiming that the West children were being kept in the cellar of the home and only brought up to be raped and sodomised. According to Fred's lawyer Howard Ogden, Anne-Marie was brought from the cellar into the main house so she could be 'broken in' by her father Fred.[58]

Thousands of video-tapes, recorded on the family's camera, were confiscated by the investigators. As police went through the tapes, some of them showed the family on outings. Others showed Rose servicing clients from a bedroom in the West home, while yet more showed young women being raped and tortured during violent bondage sessions. The police had enough evidence to remove the children from the West household.

Fred was arrested for the molestation of Anne-Marie on August 6, 1992 and was charged to face trial. He pleaded not guilty to the charges. Before the trial could proceed, Anne-Marie withdrew the complaints of rape and sodomy and refused to testify against her father. Later, once the 'House of Horrors' had been uncovered, police realised why she had done so. She did not want to end up under the house, like so many others over the years.

While viewing the tapes, DC Hazel Savage began working out the family tree of the West children, and noticed that there were gaps. Heather West was noticeably missing from the family videos after 1987. When the younger children were interviewed about the whereabouts of their older sister, many of them told them of the family joke 'that Heather was buried under the patio'.[59] After 18 months of looking for any evidence of Heather alive, police decided that she was indeed dead, probably buried at the house as the West children had joked.

Savage and four other officers arrived at 25 Cromwell St, with a search warrant, on Thursday 14 February 1994. Mae West answered the front door to find Detective Hazel Savage standing on the stoop. 'Mum, she's here again,' the young woman called out, towards the lounge room. Rosemary West moved from the lounge, where she was watching an Australian soap opera, to the front door, wearing little more than a t-shirt. The house was a mess and its residents were in a similar state of disarray. So, began the discovery of one of the world's worst serial murder and child abuse cases.

The warrant explained that officers were there to search the back garden for the body of Heather West. The police officers believed that 16-year-old Heather had been murdered by her parents in 1986 or 1987. Rosemary told officers they were harassing her and then yelled to her adult step-daughter Anne-Marie to call Fred, who was working on a nearby building site. Rose took the phone from Anne-Marie and barked down the line at her husband,

'Police are digging the garden up, come home quick.'[60] The House of Horrors was about to be uncovered.

When Fred arrived home, he was taken straight to the local police station by DC Savage. He calmly told her that he had 'nothing to bloody hide'.[61] When faced with the children's comments about the family joke, Fred mocked police for acting on such a whim. He appeared confident that the true horrors of 25 Cromwell Street would remain hidden.

Both Rose and Fred told police the same story about Heather's whereabouts, claiming she had run away with a female lover. They said they hadn't seen her in years and did not know her current whereabouts, and continued with their story. Meanwhile, police began to dig up the yard. The couple were released home for what would be their final evening together. Fred decided that he would confess to killing Heather in the hopes that police would stop digging.

The following day, Fred admitted to police that on 19 June 1987, while Rosemary was out, he'd had an argument with Heather and struck her across the face. He told police that when she laughed at him, he 'brought [his] two hands up and grabbed her round the neck'[62] and squeezed until she stopped moving. He claimed that he then tried to revive her by stripping her naked, placing her in the bathtub and running cold water over her, in the hope that the shock of the cold would wake her. When that failed, he dismembered her.

He went into detail about the way he cut up his daughter's body: 'I looked around everywhere to try and find a knife or something … I looked at the axe … there was no way I could touch … her with it. I just couldn't do it. So, I saw this knife sticking out with two prongs on the end … and I got that and I tried it with the big ones (bones) first and it was terrible … I finally managed to take her head off and then her legs. That was unbearable.'[63] The description was gruesome and shocking, yet Fred told it as though he was reading a story and not reliving his daughter's brutal murder. He said that after dismembering her, he put the pieces of his daughter into a garbage bag, and buried Heather's body in the garden after the rest of the West family had retired for the night.

For the next three days, as forensic experts continued to dig at Cromwell Street, investigators tried to get Fred to talk, specifically asking him if there were any other bones in the garden. After a lengthy pause, he replied, 'That's a peculiar question.'[64] He maintained that they would only find Heather's bones. Then the investigators explained to Fred the problem they had with his story: Heather didn't have three legs.[65] When they told him they'd uncovered a third leg bone, and asked him who it belonged to, Fred replied, after drawing a deep breath, 'Shirley … Shirley Robinson.'[66] The House of Horrors was finally giving up its secrets.

Five days into the investigation, Fred was losing count of the number of murders he had confessed to. When describing the internment of Shirley Robinson, he told police, 'I mean where is this going to end? By this time, I am realising that that is three ... two ... that's two not three.'[67] Police knew that Fred had made a monumental error. While on a break with his lawyer away from police, he confessed to the murder of a third woman. He named her only as 'Shirley's mate' and said that she too was buried in the yard near the back step of the house.

Police took Fred back to Cromwell St, which was now swarming with media, to point out where the body was buried. From the yard, Fred could already see the uncovered body in a plastic bag in one of the holes dug by police. He later recalled, 'I looked straight across and I could see her. I think she is in a plastic bag ... you could actually see it in the corner ...'[68] According to Fred, he had strangled 'Shirley's mate' with a piece of flexible hosing.

When again left alone with his lawyers, they begged Fred to give police any further information he might have. He was told that if there had been more, he should confess. Fred looked at his defence team and said, 'There is a fucking load more.'[69] He confessed to another five murders, eventually sitting down to write out a confession. In the childish scrawl of an illiterate labourer, he wrote, 'I Frederick West ... wish to admit to a further (approx.) 9 killings, expressly, Charmaine, Reena (sic), Linda Gough, and others to be identified.'[70]

Fred, along with police investigators, returned to the house on Cromwell Street after 10pm on 5 March 51994. Down in the cellar of the terrace house, he pointed to the burial sites of six more bodies. For days, police continued to dig beneath the house and in the garden, uncovering body after body. What had begun as the search for a murdered young girl had ended up unearthing a pair of sadistic serial killers.

Yet as Fred West continued to confess to murdering his victims, he played down how he had killed them, claiming he had strangled each of them in a fit of rage, rather than during a session of sexual torture, evident in the bindings and tape that was found with many of the bodies, as well as their specific injuries and missing body parts. After months of interviews, he again changed his story. After seeing his wife in court after her own arrest on 24 April 1994, he realised she no longer considered him her partner, and knew that she would likely tell investigators her own story. Instantly, he turned on her. He told his lawyer that before he had been prepared to take the blame for all of the murders, but now he wanted to include his wife's involvement in the killings. He also told police that she was solely responsible for Heather's murder.

As the bodies continued to mount, Fred could see no possible way to escape the numerous murder charges. His wife and partner in crime had snubbed him, he was the most hated man in Britain, if not the world, and though many of his children chose to stand by him, he knew that was only temporary. On New Year's Day 1995, just before noon, Fred West was found dead in his cell. He had hanged himself with strips of his bedsheet, leaving Rose to face the murder charges alone.

Rose's trial for the sexual abuse, torture and murder of 10 of the victims opened in October 1995. She denied any knowledge of the victims that investigators had found buried beneath her family homes, yet the prosecution were quick to point out what a perfect partner she had been for her murderous husband. The pair, both of whom had committed incest with their own parents, had been a lethal combination together. Their relationship had stretched beyond the murders of wayward teens and hitchhikers to their own children. They had both ritually and systematically abused their children from very young ages, attempting to skew their offspring's' belief about such taboo practices, telling them that their early introduction into sexual abuse would in fact help them in their adult lives –possibly as they had both been told by their own parents when they were children themselves. After a lengthy trial that produced dozens of witnesses and experts, many of whom provided evidence on the horrific injuries the victims had suffered, the jury took little time in finding the serial killer guilty. Rose was sentenced to 10 life terms.

Following the conclusion of the trial, the home where many of the victims had been found was demolished and replaced with a park. The building's bricks and structures were buried at an undisclosed dumpsite to prevent macabre souvenir hunters selling the pieces.

According to David Canter, one of Britain's leading expert on criminology, the sexual atrocities and murders committed by Fred and Rose West would never have occurred had the two grown up in normal family circumstances.[71] The abuse the pair had endured themselves as children gave them both a skewed set of values, in which violent and sexual abuse was tolerated, even encouraged. During his confession, Fred claimed that his own sexual appetite and values were shaped by the sexual abuse he received in the bed of his own mother. Incestuous relationships in both Fred and Rose's childhoods would have been seen as part of daily life, something that happened in every family, according to others who have grown up with incest and sexual abuse. The normalcy of the events was cemented in the children, who would grow up to become abusers themselves. The West children all suffered sexual and physical abuse at the hands of both of their parents, so the sins of the previous two generations were passed onto the next.

The childhood depravity that made Fred and Rose killers was a great distance from the upbringing of Karla Homolka and Paul Bernardo. The young and beautiful couple were polar opposites of the dowdy and uneducated Wests, yet both couples committed strikingly similar crimes. Bernardo, like Fred West, had a voracious sexual appetite that could not be sated by normal physical practices. Though there were problems in his childhood, nothing pointed to the serial killer he would become. Also, like West, he became a rapist before moving on to murder, fooling those around him with a convincing facade of normality.

Paul Bernardo and Karla Homolka

Paul Bernardo was conceived illegitimately in Ontario, Canada, when his mother, Marilyn Bernardo, returned to the comfort of a previous boyfriend after problems in her marriage. Marilyn's husband, Kenneth Bernardo, was an abusive man who was known by neighbours to be a peeping tom. When Marilyn had found him fondling their baby daughter, she left him and sought out an ex-lover. However, she returned to live with her husband once again and Paul was born, believing Kenneth was his father. It was only years later, during a violent argument with his mother, that the teenage boy discovered the truth about his real father.

By the time he was at university, Paul had grown bored of normal sex and preferred to dominate submissive women, demanding anal sex and fellatio. He would also beat up his numerous girlfriends and urinated and defecated on them during sex.[72] In October 1987, 23-year-old Paul Bernardo was working at a large Toronto accounting firm when he met Karla Homolka.

Karla Leanne Homolka was born on 4 May 1970 in Port Credit, Ontario. She was the eldest of three daughters born to Dorothy and Karel Homolka. The family lived in St Catherines, Ontario where Karla first became interested in working with animals. While still in high school she got a part-time job working at a veterinary clinic. After leaving school she started at another clinic as a full-time veterinary assistant.

Homolka was attending a vet conference in Toronto when she was spotted by Bernardo across a room. The seventeen-year-old was besotted by the attention from the older man. He was an attractive, successful businessman in her eyes and she soon told her friends she had met the man she was going to marry. The pair spent the first night together in a hotel room having rough, fervent sex for hours. The relationship was sexually charged from the very beginning and Bernardo gave Homolka a list of demands and instructions on how she should behave and dress and things he wanted her to do for and to him.

When Bernardo failed the exam to become an accountant he decided he could earn more money in other ways and soon began trafficking stolen goods across the American/Canadian border.

After a few years together Homolka made plans for a wedding to match the fairy-tale romance she was living, even as their sexual relationship grew more sadistic. Homolka started to encourage Bernardo's deviant behaviour: 'Karla, handcuffed, on her knees and begging for him, was scratching an itch. Paul asked her what she would think if he was a rapist. She would think it was cool. Their love deepened. He started raping women in earnest' as the unidentified Scarborough rapist.[73]

From May 1987, Bernardo had savagely raped several women. He would often attack his victims from behind, grabbing them after they had stepped off a bus in a secluded area. He anally raped most his victims and forced them to perform fellatio before letting them go. One of the victims was able to get a look at her attacker and went to police with the description.

Many of Bernardo's friends made jokes about how much the picture looked like him, but a few took it seriously enough to report him to the police. Police visited Bernardo and was asked to provide saliva, blood and sperm samples for DNA comparison. However, the samples were lost.[74]

By December 1990, Karla's parents were happy that their eldest daughter had found such a handsome successful young man; Karla's younger sister Tammy was also thrilled, yet she was to become the couple's first victim.

On 23 December 1990, Bernardo slipped a few sedatives into Tammy's drinks. He was frustrated that he wasn't his fiancé's first lover and so he wanted to take Tammy's virginity. Karla held a cloth soaked in halothane over her sister's nose and mouth. Tammy passed out from the drug quickly and Bernardo began the attack. Homolka filmed the abuse while she monitored Tammy's breathing. Homolka encouraged Bernardo to rape and sodomise her sister. Bernardo pushed Homolka's face towards her sister's vagina and told her to perform cunnilingus. Homolka refused several times before Bernardo became abusive, hitting her over the back of the head as he forced her closer to her sister's vagina. Tammy began to vomit and her head lolled forward blocking her airway. Karla redressed her sister and turned her upside down in an attempt to clear her airways.

Unfortunately, Tammy fell into a coma. After hiding the videotapes, the couple called the paramedics and woke the family. The ambulance team attempted to revive the comatose girl without success. The family was questioned regarding any possibility that that Tammy had taken anything besides alcohol—she had a huge purple stain around her mouth that suggested drug ingestion. Karla and Paul claimed that Tammy had only been drinking 'screwdrivers' but had drunk quite a few. In the end, Tammy's death was declared an accident and no toxicology tests were conducted. The purple stain was explained away as an acid burn from the vomiting.

One day, in January, Bernardo made a big announcement. He told Karla's parents that he was moving out and Karla was to go with him. The pair found a house in Port Dalhousie and moved in soon after Tammy's funeral. Paul continued to earn money by smuggling cigarettes and other merchandise across the border. The money was lucrative but Karla was concerned that it would bring unwanted attention from the police.

Bernardo spent a lot of time away from their new home and continued raping women and girls he found walking home at night-time. One evening, Homolka called Bernardo's mobile phone and told him she had a gift waiting for him. Bernardo arrived home and discovered a pretty teenage girl unconscious in their house. Karla had coerced Tammy's girlfriend Jane over and drugged her. She had thought that if she could find virginal victims for her fiancé then he may stay home and perhaps treat her better. Bernardo enjoyed his gift. He first made Homolka perform cunnilingus on their sleeping victim, and then raped the girl before sodomising her. But Karla's plan did not work; it did not stop him from going out and raping victims.

On Friday 14 June 1991, Leslie Mahaffy spent the evening with friends and ignored her parents 10 p.m. curfew. Her parents had asked her to be home early and to remain in a group. The Scarborough Rapist had been attacking victims more frequently and they were naturally concerned for their daughter's safety. But Leslie did not share their worry and 10 p.m. came and went. It was not until 2 a.m. that Leslie decided it was time to head home. When she arrived at her front door she found that her parents had locked her out, in an attempt to teach her a lesson.

Bernardo spotted Leslie. He grabbed her at knifepoint as she walked by. He drove her to his house, where he forced her to strip naked as he filmed the terrified girl. He blindfolded the teenager and made her lie down. As he went to penetrate her vaginally he climaxed. Bernardo was furious at himself for ejaculating so quickly and took his anger out on the young woman, beating her savagely across her back and head. Karla heard the commotion in the lounge-room and went to see what Bernardo was doing. According to Homolka, 'We raped a little girl down here in my room. You went out and you found her. Got her. Brought her back to the house, brought her downstairs. I was shocked. I gave you that. I let you do that because I love you. Because you're the king'.[75] Bernardo was pleased that Homolka had woken up; he now had two women under his control.

He grabbed the video camera and directed his fiancé to engage in various sexual positions with their captive. Bernardo then sodomised and raped Leslie before murdering her. Her remains where encased in concrete and thrown off a bridge on Lake Gibson.[76] The same day the girl's body was found; the couple were married.

On 30 November 1991, five months after Leslie's murder, 14-year-old Terri Anderson disappeared. The young girl's naked body was found in the waters of Port Dalhousie six months later on 23 May 1992, a month after the body of the killers' third victim was found. Though no charges were ever laid for the murder of Terri, many investigators believe that Bernardo and Homolka were to blame.[77]

Kristen French was abducted on 16 April 1992 and taken to the killer couple's home. For two days she was subjected to rape, sodomy and torture before the couple murdered her. Her body was found in a ditch near the Port Dalhousie lake two weeks later.[78]

By February of 1993, Bernardo, as the Scarborough Rapist, had raped dozens of women and had murdered several teen girls, yet police were no closer to catching him. That was until Paul brutally beat Karla. She called the police and charged him with assault and battery. Using Karla as a punching bag proved to be Paul's fatal mistake. The physical abuse had been going on for years, but this time he blackened both her eyes, knocked out several teeth, and fractured several ribs. Homolka called the police who investigated the matter, taking the badly beaten woman to the hospital. Toronto detectives interviewed her at length as she began to tell them about the life she had led in the control of her sexually abusive husband. Piece by piece, the rapidly materialising jigsaw depicting Paul Bernardo as a serial killer were falling into place.

When Karla's favourite uncle arrived at the hospital she whispered to him that Paul was the Scarborough Rapist and he had killed Leslie Mahaffy and Kristen French. Bernardo was arrested on 10 February and charged with the Scarborough rapes and the murders of Leslie and Kristen. Karla became afraid of being pursued as an accomplice, so Karla made a deal where she would plead guilty to being an accomplice and received twelve years in penal servitude for each of the two victims in exchange for giving police the evidence they needed against Bernardo. Had the videotapes been viewed before the deal was made, a completely different outcome may have been achieved.

Twenty-five-year-old Homolka was convicted in 1993 of manslaughter and sentenced to twelve years in prison.[79] She was released from prison in July 2005. The Canadian government placed restrictions on her parole and she has been in the media many times since her release. Reports claim the woman, who helped murder at least two girls, is now a mother.

Thirty-one-year-old Bernardo, in the face of the evidence from his wife, pleaded not guilty. His defence was that both girls had died while he was out of the house. He claimed that Homolka was responsible for their murders.[80] However, he was found guilty of the murders and admitted to fourteen sexual assaults.[81] He was sentenced to two consecutive life terms[82] in prison, under a 'dangerous offender' classification, meaning he is to never be released. He has since been questioned about several other disappearances but he has refused to admit to any further murders.

The St Catherines home once owned by Bernardo and Homolka was torn down following the sentencing of the killers.[83]

John Glover

It began as a small newspaper article, on page seven, entitled 'Woman, 82, dies—a victim of violence.' And as each victim was discovered, the articles continued to bubble through until they surfaced on the front page of the newspapers with 'It was Lady Ashton's last walk (before she was murdered).' By that time the public in Mosman, indeed all of Sydney, was in a panic as each elderly lady was found battered and posed in lewd positions. The 'Granny Killer' was the first modern serial killer to stalk Sydney and though police would indeed catch their man, one woman would lose her life as police stood outside her door in wait.

Camelia Gardens was an apartment block on Military Road, the main arterial road through Mosman. However, the front of the building was hidden from the road. A novice of the area would have difficulty spotting the entrance; the building appeared to shy away from the noise of the street. The portico of Camelia Gardens faced to the side rather than the front of Military Road and therefore offered privacy for the comings and goings of residents, mainly the elderly, though there were families and singles residing within. The killer used the privacy for murder.

On 1 March, 1989, at 3.40pm Glover killed for the first time. When the elevator doors opened on the ground floor of the Camelia Gardens Apartments, two boys stepped out and saw a sight that remains with them still. Eighty-two-year-old Gwendolin Mitchelhill was attempting to crawl to the glass security doors at the entrance of the building. Blood dripped from the savage wounds across her head. Her stockings had been torn from her legs, her walking stick was tossed to the side and her handbag, found nearby, had been rifled through, its contents neatly set out around it. The boys quickly sought help. On such a busy road people were quick to come to the elderly woman's aid. It was assumed that Mrs Mitchelhill had fallen and hit her head. The neat arrangement of her personal items from her handbag was not seen as significant. The blood on the path was quickly washed away.

The elderly woman was rushed to the emergency ward by ambulance. One of the medics found the whole scene to be unusual for a fall. He then had a thought about the woman's bag, how it had been placed neatly with her other items. His suspicions nagged at him, so he reported the incident to Mosman police. Over the next few hours, doctors worked quickly to prevent further blood building up in Mrs Mitchelhill's brain from the severe knock. On further examination of the wound it was obvious that Mrs Mitchelhill had not simply fallen because her wounds were more consistent with a strike from a blunt instrument. Adding to her injuries were two black eyes and several broken ribs. The doctors also decided to contact Mosman police.

Mrs Mitchelhill lost her battle for life later that same evening. Mosman police sent the Physical Evidence crew and homicide detectives to investigate what was possibly a murder. A check of her handbag found that it did not contain the purse she had with her during a shopping excursion earlier in the day. The post-mortem examination conducted the next day revealed that Mrs Mitchelhill had suffered severe bruising to the right eye consistent with a fist, severe bruising to the right shoulder consistent with a blunt object, two wounds to the back of the skull consistent with a blunt object and seven broken ribs consistent with a fist.

The cause of death was attributed to her head and chest injuries which were consistent with a vicious attack. There was no evidence to suggest that Mrs Mitchelhill had been sexually interfered with. With help from the Homicide Squad from Chatswood, the Mosman detectives began investigating the assault. Someone had attacked and murdered a defenceless old woman, and police wanted to find out quickly who it was. Little did police know, but this murder would not remain isolated. Two months later another elderly woman was murdered.

On 9 May, 1989, eighty-four-year-old Lady Winfreda Ashton had a busy day. She attended an appointment at the Sydney Eye Hospital and then popped over to the Mosman RSL before leaving at around 2.30pm. She withdrew her shopping and spending money at her local bank and then busied herself at the local supermarket, stopping to talk to some friends on the way. She then started her walk home. She stopped at her mailbox and then headed towards the front entrance foyer of the units where she lived. In the foyer Lady Ashton met her killer.

Lady Ashton was found dead later that evening when another resident came down to the rubbish room. She was face down on the floor. Her shoes and walking stick, like Mrs Mitchelhill, were placed nearby. Her handbag had been opened and her purse was missing. Her injuries echoed the attack on Mrs Mitchelhill. Her autopsy report read: 'Large bruise to the head, caused by a blow, bruise to the rear of her hear consistent with her head being forced to the ground. Five left ribs were also fractured.' However, this time her death was not due to her injuries, this time the killer made sure he had finished the job before leaving. She had been strangled with her pantyhose. The marks had cut so deep that fibres were imbedded in her skin. Again, no sexual assault was evident.

Police knew that the similarities in the two attacks were alarming. Both women had suffered massive bodily injuries consistent with punching. The two crime scenes were in close proximity (only about 1km apart). Both women had their purse stolen and the attacks happened at the entrance to the victim's residence. Police decided that the two murders were linked. Now the search was on before the killer struck again. The worst problem was that robbery did not seem to be the motive; both women had little money with them. The violent attack appeared to be the reason that the killer struck so investigators sought help in trying to provide a profile of the killer. Police Consultant Dr Rod Milton, a psychiatrist, was asked to assist police in constructing a profile of the offender they sought. The information was not released to the public, but pointed to a younger killer, a loner, who was unstable. Yet this profile was way off the mark. This killer was in a group all of his own and did not fit into the usual serial killer profiles.

On 9 July, 1989, two months to the day since her murder, Lady Ashton's purse was found in, ironically, Ashton Park. The woman who found the purse, not realising the significance of it, popped it into the mailbox of Lady Ashton after checking inside for identification.

On 18 October, 1989, eighty-six-year-old Doris Cox was found in the front garden of Garrison Retirement Village where she lived. She was sitting down, calling for help, her face covered in blood. She had several large grazes on her face and she had lost a few of her teeth. Again, people who had come to the elderly woman's aid thought she had fallen and, not wanting to alarm other residents, the scene was washed down. The next day administrators mentioned the incident to police, not thinking that it could have been an attempted murder. Police quickly asked the Medical Examiner who had examined the two deceased women's bodies to check Mrs Cox's injuries. The ME concluded that they were also consistent with being attacked, possibly by the killer. Mrs Cox's injuries were from having her face rammed into the brick wall after being hit on the head from behind. Though she survived the brutal attack, Mrs Cox was unable to help police in identifying her attacker.

The next murder happened within the month. This time the killer moved to a new hunting ground in nearby Lane Cove, but it did not take police long to link it to the Mosman murders and attacks. On Thursday, 2 November, 1989, a nine-year-old girl found eighty-five-year-old Margaret Pahud along a pathway shortcut. Mrs Pahud had been out shopping during the day and had been returning home when she was attacked. The young girl alerted her mother and another neighbour who rushed to the scene. Mrs Pahud was lying face down with her head surrounded by a huge pool of blood. Someone went to a nearby doctor's office and asked for help. Mrs Pahud was unconscious, but, by the time the ambulance arrived, she had died. Before police arrived to investigate, the scene was again washed down and all traces of evidence were gone. Her bag was missing.

The post-mortem revealed striking similarities to the others. Mrs Pahud had suffered heavy blows to the rear of her head, causing a fractured skull consistent with being struck with a blunt object, and lacerations to her face and head. Mrs Pahud's bag did turn up later and was handed in to police. Only the money was missing.

A taskforce was implemented to investigate the alarming number of murders and to find the perpetrator. Leading the team was Mike Hagan and 'Miles' O'Toole. While police stepped up their investigation, the killer also raised the stakes. Within twenty-four hours of the attack on Mrs Pahud, the killer struck again. On 3 November, eighty-one-year-old Olive Cleveland was attacked from behind as she entered the Westley Gardens Retirement Village where she lived. She was found lying face down across the pathway. This time, however, the killer added to his signature. He pulled up the woman's dress to expose her legs. Her pantyhose had been removed and were tied tightly around the elderly victim's throat. Again, like the other victims, her head was surrounded by a halo of blood. Her personal items, her bag, shoes and glasses were near her feet—a nasty calling card of the killer. Again, in a hindrance to police, the blood was washed away so as not to worry the other patients of the nursing home.

The post-mortem again resembled the others. Miss Cleveland suffered bruising and lacerations around her head and body. Her skull was fractured. Miss Cleveland's death was due to the pantyhose tied around the neck three times.

Police were beginning to piece together even more clues about their killer. So far, he always struck around 3.00 in the afternoon and there were never any witnesses and, though, Mrs Pahud was out of the vicinity of the other murders, they were all still in relatively close proximity. As each day passed the police felt a sigh of relief that the killer did not strike, yet that feeling was short-lived and the worst had yet to come.

Muriel Falconer was still quite spritely for her age of ninety-three. She was often seen doing errands around Mosman, going on walks and spending time shopping along the main promenade. On 24 November, 1989, Meals on Wheels called at her home at 11.30am to deliver her food. When there was no answer a note was left, saying they would call again at 1.00pm. When she did not answer the door a second time, enquiries were made after her safety. A neighbour decided to check to make sure she was all right after not having seen her since the previous afternoon. After knocking a few times, the neighbour used the spare key to let herself in. The sight that met her sent her running for the police. Mrs Falconer was lying face down in the hallway. She had been stripped of her clothes from the waist down, and her dress and petticoat had been pulled up over her head. That did nothing to conceal the large pool of blood stemming from her wounds. Her shoes and shopping from the day before were at her feet and her purse was open.

The post-mortem revealed the same afflictions as the others in the string of murders the media dubbed the 'Granny Killings'. Mrs Falconer had been beaten and her head sustained severe injuries, including fractures in three places. Several bones in her face had been broken. Her pantyhose and the belt from her dress were wrapped tightly around her tiny throat. This time, the killer had murdered inside a victim's home. Therefore, the scene was perfectly preserved except for the neighbour and a doctor checking for any sign of life of the woman.

The police finally had a breakthrough on this case. In the hallway, the killer had stepped in the victim's blood on his exit and had left bloody footprints. These would later be checked against Glover and found to be a match, helping to cement the case against him in court. Now the case was front-page news all over Sydney with headlines such as:

- Woman, 85, dies in fourth North Shore bashing.
- 2 in 2 days: another grannie slain. Madge (Pahud) murdered on her daily walk.
- Reward doubled to 200,000 dollars to catch granny killer.
- Rush of 'Granny killer' sightings.

The police received hundreds of calls from the public and, along with Dr Milton's profile, one young man became the prime suspect. He was a known psychotic and was seen in the vicinity of several of the murders and was also picked out by witnesses in photo line-ups. The suspect was actually never eliminated from police enquiries. The taskforce responsible for the case decided to change tack. They requested from all nearby police stations, records of any elderly women being attacked. Several were forwarded to the detectives and a common description of the unknown assailant appeared. The suspect in all recent assaults had been a white male, aged about 50 years with grey hair, not the young loner they had been trying to pin the murders on. Two reports also stuck out from the rest. The first was the attack on eighty-five-year-old Margaret Todhunter. On 11 January, 1989, six weeks before the first murder, Mrs Todhunter was walking home when a man walked past her then turned behind her and struck her in the back of the head. As she fell to the ground the 'grey-haired man' grabbed her bag and fled the scene. Mrs Todhunter received a large gash to the back of her head which required eight stitches.

Her description of the man was quite thorough. She said he was male, approximately fifty years old, 5'7", grey hair, well-kept, broad shoulders, thick chest, large stomach, and wore a white business shirt and cream trousers. The second report that drew interest was the attack of eighty-two-year-old Euphemia Carnie on 25 August, 1989. When returning to her residence at North Haven Retirement Village, she was punched in the chest and knocked to the ground. Her attacker took her handbag and drove away in a blue car. She suffered severe bruising to her ribs, chest and back of the head. Her description of the assailant matched the account given by Mrs Todhunter. The two attacks were added to the five murders and one attempted murder attributed to the 'Granny Killer'. However, the numbers were to increase still.

On 11 January, 1990, Daisy Roberts, an elderly patient at Greenwich Hospital was assaulted. Mrs Roberts said that a grey-haired male entered her room and placed his hands under her nightdress and held her breasts. He explained he was checking her body heat. He then walked away. Mrs Roberts raised the alarm and hospital authorities quickly informed police of the incident. One nurse told police she had earlier spoken to the pie salesman. She had asked him why he was in an area of the hospital he shouldn't have been. The salesman was quickly found on hospital grounds and when challenged about the assault on Mrs Roberts, he denied the allegation and quickly left. The man was John Glover.

Police asked Glover to attend Chatswood detectives office at 5pm, 13 January, 1990. After waiting an hour for him to arrive, police decided to call his house. His wife answered and told them that her husband had attempted suicide and was now in Royal North Shore Hospital. The suicide note Glover had written included references to 'no more grannies' and 'Essie started it'. Little did Mrs Glover know the significance of the note's contents.

Due to his mental state, the officers were not able to interview Glover that evening and when they returned the next day he refused to make any admissions on legal advice. He did, however, admit to being at the Greenwich Hospital on 11 January.

Glover also allowed the detectives to take a Polaroid photo of him. Mrs Carnie, Mrs Roberts and Mrs Todhunter identified him as their attacker. From that point on, Glover was the main suspect in the Granny Killings. The police decided to not question Glover anymore, for fear that it may scare him off. They kept a vigil at all times as they furthered their enquiries into his background and history.

John Wayne Glover was born John Walter Glover on 26 November, 1932, to Walter and Freda in Wolverhampton, England. His mother failed dismally at being maternal and John felt unloved from a very young age. In 1935, John's brother Barry was born. By 1941, Freda and Walter had gone their separate ways. Both had been unfaithful during their marriage.

Freda gained custody of the two boys. Soon after her divorce came through, Freda remarried and had two more children, Patricia and Clifford, however Freda's new husband did not father Clifford. The family moved constantly. Sometimes the two older boys were returned to their natural father and the interruption of changing schools made John uncomfortable. He never settled into a schooling routine and subsequently achieved poor grades. In 1945, at the age of thirteen, John witnessed a friend's fall from a tree. The boy died from his injuries. This incident stayed with Glover forever. By 1946, John left school and went into full-time employment. His first job was as an apprentice electrician, however the fifteen-year-old was still unsettled by family life and he left the position due to a lack of concentration.

However, Glover found work as an offsider for an odd-jobs man and enjoyed the work. It allowed Glover to move away from home and into a share-house with friends. It was during this time that he discovered sex. He would date as many young girls as he could and would boast to friends about his sexual prowess. Glover had also begun pilfering. He would steal anything he could, often resulting in appearances in front of the magistrate. By the time he was twenty-two years old, he had several robbery charges against him, these being:

- March, 1947: Break and Enter in Wolverhampton.
- October, 1947: Theft of tools and stamps from employer.
- May, 1952: Theft of clothing from Lincoln City Club— fined £4 and made to pay £1 in compensation to the club.
- December, 1952: Stole a coat from a van before deciding to steal the entire van. He was fined £5 and disqualified from driving for 12 months.
- 1954: Stole a handbag, and with regards to his extensive record, was placed on two years' probation.

Glover also served in the British army for two years. After his national service, he was employed as a bus conductor from 1954 to 1957. It was while working as a conductor that he noticed an advertisement for qualified tram drivers and conductors in Melbourne, Australia. Glover applied and was accepted as a conductor. He arrived in Melbourne by ship in 1957 as a twenty-four-year-old. He had decided to leave the old John Glover behind; he changed his middle name to reflect his new start in life. Life settled down for a while for the young man but it was not long before the old overtook the new. On 11 September, 1962, Glover attacked seventy-three-year-old Myrtle Ince as she walked along Berrick Street in Camberwell, Victoria. The elderly woman was attacked from behind and knocked unconscious; her dress was pushed up, though no sexual assault took place. A month later, on 4 October, twenty-year-old Valerie Bird was attacked from behind at 10.30pm as she walked home in Camberwell. She screamed and a man came to her aid. The young woman's aide was able to identify Valerie's attacker as Glover. Glover was charged with indecent assault causing actual bodily harm. He also admitted to the earlier attack. Glover was given four years' probation for the two assaults.

Beginning in 1967, John Glover began seeing Jacqueline Gail Rolls, known as Gay to her friends. She was from a wealthy family and on 1 June, 1968, the happy couple married. Gay's mother, Veronica, known as Essie, did not approve of Glover. After the marriage, Glover began a job in liquor sales but was sacked for being lazy. However, Glover enjoyed working in sales and found a similar job soon after in Sydney. The couple moved into a property in the well-to-do north Sydney suburb of Mosman and settled down to married life. However, Essie and husband John moved in with the couple, building a third storey onto John and Gay's property. The relationship between Glover and Essie was strained but for the sake of Gay the pair was civil. In 1971, John and Gay were blessed with a daughter, Kellie, then another daughter, Marney, in 1973 completed the Glover family. In 1981, Glover began his final job as a pie salesman in Alexandria. He was known by fellow workers as 'smutty...a bludger and a thief.' He was a well-known face around the Mosman RSL and was a participating member of various community groups around the area. Glover was extremely house and city proud.

Then Freda, his mother, immigrated to Sydney from England, throwing the man's life into disarray. Glover had such a hatred for his mother. Once when cleaning out one of the houses during a move, he found a photo of his mother wearing nearly nothing and seductively posed. He had detested her for her loose morals but the picture had cemented his hatred of her.

He refused to allow her to stay at his Mosman home, which already housed his over-bearing mother-in-law; so, he shipped her off to a nearby hotel. He would begrudgingly take his daughters to see Freda, but would leave as soon as he could. Then in 1988, life changed for John Glover forever; a change that would send him down a path of murder and violence.

Glover was diagnosed with breast cancer, a rare but not unheard-of diagnosis for a male. Glover saw this as a female-only disease and took the news quite badly, taking it out on the family. Essie was sent to a nursing home when Gay could no longer nurse her as well as Glover. Freda, Glover's mother, became ill soon after and was hospitalised. Glover was the last person to see her alive on 7 October, 1988. The attacks on the elderly women of Mosman began only three months later.

Ten days after the attack on Mrs Todhunter, Essie Rolls died at the nursing home. The weight of the deaths seemed to have been a catalyst for the Granny murders. It appeared that Glover had hated his mother for leaving his father and re-marrying three times and he also had a deep-seated hatred for his mother-in-law. The 'Essie did it' quote in Glover's suicide note was blaming his mother-in-law for his murderous rampage.

Police now needed hard evidence against Glover. Surveillance was set up and police watched as he drove through Mosman. Glover was unaware of the surveillance, often stopping his car, getting out and wandering along the streets of Mosman looking for victims.

Police decided to use a newly invented tracking device that was currently being trialled in surveillance. With permission from the pie company Glover worked for, police had the Quiktrack tracking device fitted to Glover's vehicle. That way, with Glover's roving work and extra activities, they never lost sight of him. When police returned to Royal North Shore Hospital to ask staff and patients further questions about the assault on Mrs Roberts, a break and a failure in the case happened at the same time. One receptionist interviewed stated that she was in fact John Glover's wife and that he had denied all the allegations. She also said she would tell her husband that police were questioning the hospital about him. Detectives knew then that they needed to move a little quicker; they feared that he might quieten down. But this was not the case. On 19 March, 1990, four days after their talk with Mrs Glover, police tracked Glover all over Mosman and Balmoral; it was obvious he was on the hunt. At 10.30am he stopped his car, fixed his hair, put on a tie, grabbed a briefcase and entered a dwelling. Police first assumed that he was meeting with his solicitor so they sat outside and waited. Later in the afternoon, two boys attempted to enter the same property. When they found the gate locked, they got a neighbour to help them to no avail. A dog inside the premises was barking continuously. Something was wrong. Using the dog as a reason to investigate, police went to the door to question the occupant about the dog's barking. The door was locked so they went to the rear of the property and, through a glass door, could see a hammer and what looked to be blood on the carpet of the front landing. Police then forced the front entry to investigate. The body of Joan Sinclair was found just inside the door. Near the body was a bloodstained claw hammer. Mrs Sinclair's head was wrapped in a towel and her lower clothes had been removed. Again, her pantyhose were tied around her neck.

Detectives knew they needed to be careful; Glover must still be in the house. The killer was found in the bathroom; he was semi-conscious and naked in the bath. Glover was vomiting and moaning and his face was partially submerged in the water. Paramedics were called, and Glover was treated for an alcohol and drug overdose.

Glover was moved to Royal North Shore Hospital and placed under police guard. Mrs Sinclair's post-mortem report stated that she had suffered multiple head wounds from a blunt object— the claw hammer found at the scene. Though there was much dissimilarity between the Sinclair murder and the Granny Killings, there was enough evidence to suggest they were all linked. In hospital on 20 March, 1990, Glover was briefly interviewed about the murders of the six women and the attempted murder of Mrs Cox. Glover admitted to committing each murder and the attempted murder. Later that day, Glover was formally charged with the murder of Mrs Sinclair and the police officers planned for further interviews on his discharge from hospital.

On 28 March, 1990, Glover appeared at the Glebe Coroners Court where he was formally charged with fourteen offences: six counts of first-degree murder, one count of attempted murder, one count of robbery with wounding, one count of robbery, four counts of indecent assault and one count of assaulting a female. During his trial Glover claimed that he 'felt detached, as though [he] was witnessing ... not doing it'. On Friday, 29 November, 1990, Glover was found guilty on all counts and sentenced to prison for the term of his natural life, with the recommendation that he was never to be released. Glover showed little emotion as Justice Woods passed sentence.

On 9 September, 2005, the Granny Killer committed suicide. The killer was found hanging from the grill of his prison cell.

Robert Thompson and Jon Venables

To kill a child is one of the most heinous crimes known to man. For human beings, one of the only species that murders its own without cause, it is unconscionable that we would want to cause harm to children. What is even more incomprehensible is that a killer might be a small child himself. Since the murder of Jamie Bulger hit the media, it has remained in the minds of Britons, more than 20 years after the crime. Barely a month goes by without an article about the case or the killers.

A child killing another, though rare, was not entirely without precedence. Jon Venables and Robert Thompson, the killers of two-year-old James, were not the first children in England to kill another. Child killer Mary Bell's crimes preceded James' murder by more than 25 years. The case roused public shock and revulsion in much the same way as the Bulger murder, as experts and families tried to comprehend how a child could torture and kill another. The murder committed by Venables and Thompson is often juxtaposed with the murders of Mary Bell, and from what we know of the two 10-year-old boys, the Bell case was different. Bell was the daughter of a prostitute who was forced to service her mother's clients. Having become disassociated from the abuse she'd suffered, she reacted to those who tried to get close to her with pure rage. Unable to understand the trauma she herself had endured, she inflicted harm on those around her, and the day before her 11th birthday strangled four-year-old Martin Brown. She then mutilated and murdered three-year-old Brian Howe two months later. Like James Bulger's killers, Mary Bell was granted anonymity for life, following a sentence of penal servitude at her Majesty's pleasure.

In the case of Thompson and Venables, both children came from broken homes and suffered 'great social and emotional deprivation. They grew up in an atmosphere of matrimonial breakdown, where they were exposed to, saw, heard or suffered abuse, drunkenness and violence ... [there was] no doubt that both boys saw video films frequently, showing violent and aberrant activities.'[84]

Jon Venables was born on 13 August 1982 to Susan and Neil Venables. The boy was the second of three children and lived in Walton, near Liverpool, not the poorest suburb, but far from privileged. His older brother had several disabilities, including a cleft palate, communication problems and anger issues. Venable's younger sister had learning and developmental problems.[85] His parents separated just after the birth of his sister, but continued to share the responsibility for raising the children. Jon spent half the week with his father and half the week with his mother. It was far from an ideal arrangement, but worked for the family, for the most part.

At his father's home, Venables was allowed to watch adult horror films.[86] A piece of evidence not shown at trial was a graphic

picture drawn by Jon Venables after he had watched the film
Halloween. He wrote a description to go with the picture that
described how the man was killing his victims in the film. The
picture alone is chilling, with a knife-wielding, large-breasted killer
standing amid his victims, who are splayed around him with blood
gushing from their many stab wounds. Though it is not unusual for
small boys to enjoy playing with guns and pretending to shoot each
other in the playground, the drawing was the work of a child who
had been exposed to violent ideas and images. He wrote that the
killer in his drawing was a man, but then feminised the figure by
giving it large breasts.

Venables had no fear of teachers or school principals or even
his father. The only person he feared was his mother, who would
subject him to regular beatings.[87] The possibility that Venables was
projected his mother onto the main character in *Halloween* was later
raised by author Blake Morrison, who stated that 'the drawing
suggests how seeing *Halloween* deeply disturbed an already deeply
disturbed little boy'.[88] Was Venables demonising his mother in the
picture? Juxtaposing the monster with the physical punishment he
suffered at his mother's hands? His mother was often worse the
wear for drink, and police were called when Venables and his
siblings were left home alone during her drunken binges at the local
pub. Venables was known to kick other children in the shins if he
did not get his way, but when other parents called his mother to

complain, she would hurl abuse back at them. Dr Susan Bailey described him at his trial as a boy of average intelligence, who could distinguish right from wrong.[89]

Robert Thompson was born on 23 August 1982. Most children at school knew him as an unfeeling thug from an early age; later, while Venables often cried during the court trial, Thompson rarely showed interest. He was the fifth of seven boys in the home, and survived by acting the way his older siblings did –beatings filtered down from the older children to the younger ones. Early in his childhood, Thompson was often punished by his father, who would use a belt to beat the boys while he shouted obscenities at them. Once he left, Ann Thompson was unable to cope with the boisterous children and turned to drink, spending her days at the pub. She had also been severely beaten by her husband, including suffering a miscarriage during one horrific row.

A report into the family unit likened it to 'survival of the fittest' or *Lord of the Flies*. The boys all picked on the sibling that was the next youngest to them, from the 20-year-old to the eight-year-old, and Thompson was often bullied by his brothers for sucking his thumb. They were in and out of state care after bite marks and brutal beatings were reported to welfare agencies, and most of the time, the gang of rag-tag siblings had to fend for themselves. Thompson was often seen wandering the streets in the early hours of the morning. Like Venables, his psychological assessment at trial described him as a boy of good or at least average intelligence who knew the difference between right in wrong, and he has since displayed signs of post-traumatic stress when revisiting the crime in therapy. Venables, is said to be inconsolable whenever someone mentions the murder.[90]

During their trial, Venables and Thompson, then aged 11, sat with their lawyers and social workers.[91] The days were cut to run shorter than a school day and regular breaks were offered to the young offenders, who sat playing with the ties they were told to wear in court. Venables would often cry during the testimony of witnesses and experts, looking to his parents for comfort. Thompson's parents were not there. While Venables mother tried to explain that her son followed another bad egg, his father, others would tell a different story. A teacher who testified at trial stated that Venables had once tried to choke a fellow classmate with a ruler pressed against the child's throat. His violence struck without warning and it took the teacher all of their strength to get the 10-year-old to let go. Venables had also changed schools to escape bullying.[92]

Thompson and Venables, though now forever linked due to the heinous murder, did not start out as friends. Thompson would pick on the cry-baby Venables and push him around. It was only when the two of them, both suffering from learning difficulties, were kept back a year and placed in the same class that they became friends. They quickly began truanting together.

Venables was the one who chose for James to die that fateful day on 12 February 1993. The two 10-year-olds planned to play hooky from school, go to the local shopping centre and steal a young child. It was a chilling prospect on its own for two children. The boys were truanting for the fourth time together that year; on a previous occasion, Venables' father had caught them and managed to grab his son, but Thompson escaped, taunting his friend's father as he ran off.

On this occasion, the two boys headed to the local Strand shopping centre in Bootle, Merseyside. It was a Friday, and the centre was full of mothers, busily running errands before their children came home from school, as well as many local unemployed people, who had little else to do. With a hundred shops in the small centre, there were plenty of places to get into mischief and cause strife.

Thompson thought it would be fun to steal a young child away from his mother, take the child to the nearest busy road and throw them out into the traffic. While waiting for the right child to come along, the two boys caused mischief in every store they visited. They spent their day stealing an odd assortment of items, including batteries, model paint and a few toys, but soon even stealing bored them.

They chose a first victim and managed to get the little toddler's attention, luring him away from his mother by showing him the toys they had stolen. The boys could not believe that they were going to be successful, but their elation turned to disappointment as the toddler's mother sprinted to the entrance of the store and grabbed her little boy, shocked that he had managed to get so far from her so quickly.

A pregnant Denise Bulger was also shopping at the centre, with her two-year-old son James, her brother's fiancé Nicolas and her little girl. They had a few errands to run, including getting meat and groceries for the evening's meal. James, the cute toddler, was restless. By the time they'd been to Marks and Spencers, the supermarket and the butchers, he'd had enough of shopping. For a Friday, A. R. Tyrns Butchers was quite busy, and Denise had to wait in a queue to be served. Blonde-haired and blue-eyed James played at her feet. He was wearing a thick overcoat to protect him from the outside elements. He complained that he wanted to go home to Kirkby, and Denise promised her little boy that after they bought some lamb chops for their dinner, they would go home.

Standing on the upper level of the shopping centre, Jon Venables and Robert Thompson looked out over the lower level. They spotted their next target, James. The toddler was leaning against the entrance to the butchers. The child had taken a few steps away from his mother and was occupied with something else, unaware that two predators had fixed on him. At the same time that James had taken those few steps from his mother's side, Denise was paying for their supper. She had taken her attention away from her son for only a moment, explaining to the cashier that they had given her the wrong order, but it was enough for the two 10-year-old boys to pounce.

The time was 3.43pm. Denise turned and looked down, expecting her son to be at her side. He was not there. She looked around at those still waiting to be served and then toward her future sister-in-law and niece who were waiting outside. James was not with them. That panic that only a parent can know quickly set in. The expectation of seeing her son, who must only have wandered a few steps away, soon dissipated. James was nowhere to be seen.

The customers around Denise quickly realised that her little boy had wandered off. People started looking for the toddler, as Denise made her way to the centre's management office, to get them to make an announcement. It had only taken a minute for the two boys to take James to the upper level and out an exit door. Thirty-nine seconds later, they had left the centre altogether, whilst Denise and others searched for James.

The toddler's journey to his death at the hands of two children lasted for two-and-a-half miles over two hours. Several witnesses saw James with the two boys. When questioned, the boys would tell people they had found him and were taking him to the local police station. No one confronted them when they headed in the opposite direction. One witness claimed to have seen the two boys dragging James, who was now extremely distressed and calling for his mother, part of the way. Another saw the two boys drag James towards the railway bridge and heard one of them say that they hated having a little brother. A 14-year-old girl saw one of the boys run up the hill that led to the railway line and thought, at the time, that the toddler was laughing.

Over the centre's intercom system, a disjointed voice asked all customers to look for the little boy. For the next few hours, customers and employees of the Strand searched every corner, looking for what a lost, possibly sleeping little boy. With stores closing, police were now on the scene, and several store owners were asked to return and look again, in the hopes that the little boy might be locked inside.

If they had looked at the security footage, which was not reviewed until much later, they would have seen holding one of the 10-year-olds hands, with the other boy dawdling in front of the pair, James being led from the centre hours earlier. The boys did not run, and did not look worried or concerned. They looked like they were with their younger brother. As James' father said in his book, *My James*, 'they knew what they were doing was wicked ...'[93]

No one had any idea of the horror that James was enduring while they remained at the shopping centre. Even as police, employees and family members continued the search, darkness having fallen over the suburbs, James already lay dead, more than two kilometres away, having suffered 42 separate injuries in a period of prolonged torture. The toddler had received 22 injuries to his head and a further 20 to his body. The boys had used an iron rod and 27 bricks to beat and stone him, before leaving his body on train tracks to be run over by a train and cut in two. [94]

The 'baby', as the two child killers called him in their statements, had suffered a horrendous ordeal. He had his nappy removed during the final assault and his foreskin had been violently retracted, exposing the glans of his penis. James had had batteries forced into his mouth and injuries to his rectum, suggesting that they had attempted to insert the batteries into his anus as well. The little boy's left eye had been rubbed with blue model paint the boys had stolen earlier and he had several large gashes to his forehead and skull. He had been hit to the face and mouth and a large wound to his cheek was consistent with being kicked; James' blood was on the shoes Thompson wore that day. When the severed body was found, it was surrounded by several bricks that had been thrown at the toddler, all of them covered in blood splatter. Finally, he was struck with a 10kg iron bar, which killed him.

On the afternoon of the murder, Venables's mother had gone to school to pick him up, as she sometimes would, and found he had missed school that day. She went looking for him along the railway line, where she knew the boys had made a cubby house. She stopped looking for him after a few hours, knowing he would eventually turn up at home when he got hungry. She was not worried about her son, but was angry that he had missed another day of school. When he did turn up, she took him to the local constabulary to shake some sense into him for truanting from school.

The weekend after the murder, Venables was quiet and subdued as the family watched the local news, which showed grainy images of two young boys leading the missing toddler away. It wasn't long before police knocked on the doors of the both families.

While being interviewed, the two boys exhibited disturbing behaviour of how the torture and murder of the toddler had affected them. Venables cried hysterically, lashing out at family who were there to support him. He refused to admit what he had done with his mother in the room, knowing such an admission would provoke her wrath. It was only once she had told that she would still love him that he admitted his involvement. Thompson, during his initial interview, remained stoic and showed little emotion.

The subsequent trial made international news as the two boys faced a backlash of public hatred. Questions were asked of the parents regarding how they could raise such 'evil' children. The world mourned the terrible death of the toddler with the big blue eyes while demonising the two had committed the crimes. Calling the two boys 'evil' was society's way of distancing themselves from what they didn't understand. The idea of two 'bad seeds' or rotten apples was easier to contemplate than the possibility that a person could commit such atrocities without being either bad or mad.

In Britain, with 10 being the age of criminal responsibility, both boys were accountable for the murder and were found to understand that what they had done was wrong. During their lengthy journey with James, as he fought them and begged to go back to his mother, there was not a moment in which the two killers thought just to abandon him. They had committed themselves not only to the kidnapping, but to the murder as well.

On 24 November 1993, Thompson and Venables were convicted for the murder and abduction of James Bulger. They were detained at Her Majesty's pleasure and the trial judge recommended that a period of no less than eight years be served. He stated that 'very great care will have to be taken before either defendant is allowed out into the general community. Much psychotherapeutic, psychological and educational investigation and assistance will be required.'[95]

Jon Venables had been released and was living under a new identity when, in July 2010, he was arrested and sent back to prison for breaching the good behaviour clause that governed his life. Police had found pornographic images of children on his home computers. At the time, police were investigating reports of an online child porn ring, and Venables, living under his new identity, was arrested. To date, co-offender Robert Thompson has slotted into his new, anonymous life without problems.

Marybeth Tinning

Marybeth Tinning was born Marybeth Roe to parents Alton and Ruth on 11 September 1942, in Duanesburg, New York. The first of two children, Marybeth spent most of her childhood being told by family that she was unwanted and unloved. Her younger brother was the focus of the family, while Marybeth was shunned.[96] She was isolated from those around her, often being locked in a bedroom for entire days. The only attention she received was physical abuse at the end of her father's flyswatter. She later recalled that if she cried, he would lock her in a closet.[97] In court, she testified about her unhappy childhood and the abuse she suffered, saying, 'My father hit me with a flyswatter because he had arthritis and his hands were not of much use. And when he locked me in my room I guess he thought I deserved it.'[98] She was extremely loneliness as a child and attempted suicide multiple times while growing up.

At school, she was an outsider who did not fit in, and had few friends. Most of the studies were unaware that her 'strangeness' was due to a lack of social skills, which should have been taught in a caring home environment. Her loneliness at home and school was reinforced by ongoing outbursts of aberrant behaviour. She would act out, knowing that it was one way in which she would get the attention she so desperately desired.

Tinning graduated from Duanesburg High School, where her only achievement was being elected president of the Future Homemakers of America Club,[99] a social club for those who wanted to be stay-at-home mothers following their educational requirements. After high school, she worked in several menial jobs, including as a nurse's aide at Ellis Hospital, as a waitress with Flavorland, and as a local bus driver.[100]

She said later that there were only two things that she ever wanted in life: 'to be married to someone who cared for me and to have children.'[101] Her wish would come true by the time she was 22, after she went on a blind date with Joe Tinning. By 1965, the couple had married, and in May 1967 they were blessed with their first baby, Barbara. For once in her life, happiness had found Tinning. She doted on her newborn and many visitors came to see her and her baby daughter. In January 1970, they welcomed a second baby, a son they named Joseph Junior.

Though Tinning enjoyed the attention she received from those who came to coo over her children, she was still denied her parents' love. Her father Alton had become ill and spent a lot of time in hospital. Tinning, being the dutiful daughter went to see him regularly but was always spurned.[102] In October 1971, while Tinning was heavily pregnant with her third child, Alton died of a massive heart attack. Having always been cold and abusive, Marybeth had hoped her father would show her love before the end, but it never came, and his sudden death caused far-reaching psychological issues from which she would never recover. She found that the sympathetic interest from others she received at his funeral was what she had yearned for her entire life, and so learned that death would bring her what she desired most: attention.

The day after Christmas 1971, Marybeth gave birth to her third child, a daughter named Jennifer. By now, those who had supported Tinning after her father's death in October had returned to their own lives, and were busy with Christmas. Tinning went back to feeling rejected and alone. Then death struck her family once again. On 3 January 1972, the Tinnings rushed their newborn baby girl to Schenectady Hospital, where she was diagnosed with meningitis.[103] Multiple congenital brain abscesses were also found.[104] The eight-day-old baby died in hospital.

Once back at home, before the funeral, Tinning washed all of Jennifer's clothes and packed them away. She also disassembled the cot and packed up the baby's toys. The cleaning and packing up would later become part of Tinning's post-death ritual.[105] Friends and relatives again flocked to the heartbroken woman, to console her and help with her two surviving children.

As the attention began to wane, tragedy struck the Tinning family once again. Seventeen days after Jennifer's death, Tinning rushed her two-year-old son Joseph Junior to the hospital. She told medical staff he had had a seizure and he was placed under close monitoring and observation for several hours. When nothing could be found to account for the seizure, he was discharged home. Several hours later, Tinning returned with Joseph's limp body in her arms. She told doctors he had had a seizure again, causing the cot's blankets to wrap around his body and suffocate him. His death was attributed to cardiopulmonary arrest.[106] Again, she returned home to wash the toddler's clothes and pack away his belongings, and people flocked to be with her, deeply saddened and shocked two tragedies so close together, so soon after the death of her father.

On 1 March 1972, Tinning again rushed to the hospital with a child in her arms, claiming that four-year-old Barbara had had several convulsions at home. Once again, the child was monitored and doctors could find nothing wrong. Barbara was discharged into the care of her mother and the following day, Tinning returned with the child, who was unconscious. She subsequently died, without regaining consciousness. Doctors diagnosed the rare disease of Reyes Syndrome, which can cause encephalopathy (swelling of the brain), but no final conclusive evidence or testing was sought. Tinning later recalled the death, in her own warped memories: 'While we were sleeping, she called out to me and I went in and she was having a convulsion. I guess I don't even remember whether we took her by ambulance or whether we took her, but anyway we got there and they did whatever they did.' As she had done following Jennifer and Joseph's deaths, Tinning washed and packed away all of Barbara's belongings, well-wishers and mourners returned to the Tinning house to care for the grieving mother.

After Barbara's death, Tinning began working as a waitress, finding herself alone and childless again. A month after Barbara's death, Marybeth and Joe decide to contact the Department of Social Services to express an interest in becoming foster parents. Looking at the tragic circumstances that had surrounded the family, the department understood the couple's desire to foster, rather than risk whatever condition had killed their own children. By the end of 1972, the Tinnings had fostered Robert, but he moved on in January 1973. They then took in another foster child, Linda, in 1973, but she was returned when the couple found out they were expecting another child. Timothy was born on 21 November 1973, but the joy of the new baby was short-lived. The couple rushed nine-day-old Timothy to the hospital, where he was pronounced dead on arrival. His death was declared to be from Sudden Infant Death Syndrome (SIDS).

The deaths of Joe and Marybeth's children started to chip away at the solid foundation of their marriage. They started fighting over money and Marybeth's failing mental health. Joe convinced his wife to seek psychiatric attention and she was admitted to hospital, but soon after escaped and returned home.

Feeling she had also been abandoned by her husband, she attempted to poison him with the barbiturate Phenobarbital, but Joe survived and told doctors that he had attempted suicide.[107]

The couple called police in January 1974, claiming that they had been burgled, but suspicion later fell on Marybeth, following the theft of a family member's money. In late 1974, she confessed to a co-worker that she was pregnant again, and that, 'God told her to kill this one too.'[108] On 30 March 1975, Tinning gave birth to her fifth child, Nathan. While everyone around them hoped the fates of Tinning's previous four children would not fall to Nathan, it was not to be. On 20 September 1975, while Marybeth was out shopping with the baby, he died. According to Marybeth, she was driving to the store when he stopped breathing while in his car seat. She drove to St Clare's hospital with the dead baby in her arms. Like Joseph, Nathan's death was attributed to SIDS and listed as acute pulmonary oedema.

For three years, the Tinning couple tried to move on from the tragedies that had struck them. They stopped having any children for a time, nor did they foster any others. But in August 1978, the couple began adoption proceedings for newborn Michael and in October had their sixth biological child, Mary Frances. At three months old, Mary Frances was rushed to hospital unconscious, but doctors were able to successfully revive her. Her condition was listed as 'aborted SIDS'[109] and she was soon released home. A month later, she was again rushed to hospital in cardiac arrest, and doctors revived the child once more, but she was left with permanent brain damage. Mary Frances remained on life support for two days before dying.

On 19 November 1979, Tinning gave birth to Jonathan. At four months old, he was rushed to St Clare's Hospital, unconscious. He was revived but sent to a trauma hospital for further tests. When no diagnosis could be established, he was discharged. A few days later, he was again brought unconscious, and after fighting for life on a respirator for a month, died.

Though the family seemed to be cursed, the suspicion that a genetic anomaly was to blame was set aside when an adopted child also died in similar circumstances. Tinning's two-year-old adopted son Michael was taken to a paediatrician on 2 March 1981, Marybeth claiming that the child would not wake up. The toddler was already dead when doctors examined him. Suspicion at last fell on Tinning, though no charges were laid.

For the next four years, the couple remained childless, as the rumours and innuendo died down. Then on 22 August 1985, Tinning gave birth to Tami Lynne. Four months later, the baby was dead. Instead of going to hospital, Tinning went screaming to a neighbour, who came inside to find the baby dead on the changing table. After the deaths of nine children in 13 years, police were called to investigate.

In April 1986, following tests on the baby's corpse, Tinning and her husband were arrested and questioned over the baby's death. Once in custody, Marybeth broke down and told police that she believed that she was not worth 'anything in life'.[110] She confessed to three of the murders, but vehemently denied murdering the others. In her handwritten confession, she wrote, 'I did not do anything to Jennifer, Joseph, Barbara, Michael, Mary Frances, Jonathon. Just these three: Timothy, Nathan and Tami. I smothered them each with [sic] pillow because I'm not a good mother.'[111] She was charged only with the murder of Tami Lynne.

At her trial, Medical Examiner Dr Michael Baden, an expert in SIDS deaths, explained to the court, 'About three babies in a thousand die from crib death. The odds against two crib deaths in one family are enormous. The odds against three are astronomical … There is no known genetic disease that can cause sudden death in healthy children … A baby will not suffocate from being snarled in blankets and bed sheets.'[112]

After a six-week trial, Tinning was found guilty of the murder of Tami Lynne and sentenced to 20 years to life for the killing. According to experts who testified at her trial, she was a narcissist who was motivated by the attention she gained from their tragic deaths.

She has been refused parole since her eligibility in 2007. At a 2011 parole hearing, when asked what insights she had gained about herself, she replied, 'When I look back I see a very damaged and just a messed up person and I have tried to become a better person while I was here, trying to be able to stand on my own and ask for help when I need it … sometimes I try not to look in the mirror and when I do, I just, there is no words that I can express now. I feel none. I'm just, just none.'[113]

Dylan Klebold and Eric Harris

People have referred to the coming together of the two Columbine killers, Eric Harris and Dylan Klebold, as a perfect storm. A mother of one of the survivors explained that Klebold had befriended the loner Harris; Klebold was friends with lots of people, but in Harris he saw something special. Harris, in turn, saw something in Klebold. He believed he could mould the boy into a killing machine, who would help him act out his final assault on 20 April 1999, as part of a plan to 'kick natural selection up a few notches'.[114]

The Columbine High School massacre, though mostly know as a high school shooting, was meant to be, according to the diaries of the killers, a bombing to rival Timothy McVeigh's act of terrorism. And like the Oklahoma bombing, the attack was orchestrated by two people, one wielding a powerful influence over the other.

A relationship between murderers, in which one participant is more powerful than the other or others, has occurred through time immemorial. In the case of the Menendez brothers, the dominant older brother forced the younger to participate in the killing of their parents. The murders of members of the Clutter family in 1959, immortalised in Truman Capote's *In Cold Blood*, were committed by two young men – while Richard Hickock planned the murders, the weaker partner, Perry Smith, conducted them at the behest of his dominant friend. The Snowtown killings, already discussed, saw the collusion of a stronger man with other, weaker killers, who helped him commit at least 11 murders. The list goes on, and the Columbine killers were no different. Eric Harris was the mastermind and planner; he bought the weapons, he designed the bombs, and he was the boy with the plan. Klebold was his suicidal friend, caught up in the fantasy, who believed he had nothing left to live for.

In the Boston Marathon bombings of 15 April 2013, we saw a similar scenario. At the time of writing, early reports indicate that Tamerlan, the older brother, was a boxer, who allegedly had charges for domestic assault against his name. He openly claimed he had no American friends and couldn't understand the culture of his adopted homeland.[115] His younger brother, Dzhokhar, who led police on a door-to-door manhunt. was described by friends as a person who 'fit in with everyone',[116] and public opinion holds that the elder brother must have convinced him to participate.

In chilling similarity to other charismatic leaders, like Jim Jones and Charles Manson, the few friends Eric Harris had said he was 'charismatic, an eloquent speaker, well-read, the kind of guy who could bullshit for hours about anything and be witty and brilliant.'[117] Yet Harris, a young teen who had studied the Oklahoma bombing and was shocked to learn that Timothy McVeigh did not stay to watch his bombs explode, wrote in his journals that his plans would be far grander than what McVeigh had achieved. He wrote about the varying levels of carnage he wanted, and hoped the bombs he planned to set off around his high school would kill hundreds.[118]

Both Harris and Klebold kept diaries leading up to the murders, which gave police the best insight into their intentions on that fateful April day in. The massacre was not hatched as an overnight plan – they had planned it for more than a year. Their diaries detailed their collection of weapons, and videos show them practising with the high-powered shotguns and rifles they planned to use. Looking back even further than a year, there were hints of what was to come. Almost 10 years before the massacre, at the age of eight, Eric Harris had already written his first list of people to kill. He would later create a website that he used to discuss his murderous fantasies.

In January 1998, Harris and Klebold were arrested for breaking into an electronics van and stealing $400 worth of equipment; both boys were on parole at the time of the shooting. Harris later wrote that he thought the owner of the van deserved to die for being so stupid as to leave it where it could be robbed. Their friends also knew that the boys had a key to the computer rooms at school and had stolen various pieces of computer equipment.

A year before the April 1999 massacre, Harris chatted in online chatrooms about what he hoped to achieve. On April 29,

1998, Harris wrote, 'Sometime in April next year, me and V [Klebold] will get revenge and we'll kick natural selection up a few notches. We've learned the art of making time bombs, we'll set hundreds of them around roads, bridges, buildings and gas stations, anything that can cause damage and chaos. It'll be like the L.A. Riots, the Oklahoma bombing, WWII, Vietnam, Duke and Doom all mixed together … I want to leave a lasting impression on the world.'[119] Harris certainly had grand plans. Harris used the codename NBK to talk about the massacre he planned, a reference to film *Natural Born Killers*, in which a couple found fame by killing their way across America. Harris wrote: 'NBK came quickly. Everything I see and hear, I relate to NBK somehow. It feels like a god-damned movie sometimes.'[120]

Harris also made a new kill list, which included the name of a boy from high school. The student, Brooks Brown, had seen a web page entry, written by Harris, which read: 'I will rig up explosives all over town and detonate each one of them at will after I mow down a whole fucking area full of you snotty ass rich mother fucking high strung godlike attitude having worthless pieces of shit whores. I don't care if I live or die in the shootout, all I want to do is kill and injure many of you pricks as I can, especially a few people like Brooks Brown.'[121] Brooks notified his father, who told the authorities. A formal complaint was made, but police lost the documentation, and it was only after the massacre that they investigated. The boy, who survived the massacre, later reflected that police could have stopped the spree. He called it part of the perfect storm, in which many factors culminated to allow them to carry out their violent spree.[122] Brooks had also seen Harris and Klebold experiment with black powders and pipe bombs. A friend prior to the online threats, he had filmed their tests for them, as they blew up tree stumps and shot at trees on the outskirts of town.

Six weeks before the shooting, Harris' parents took him to see a doctor, who prescribed the antidepressant medication Zoloft. But Harris' condition deteriorated and his outbursts became violent. He was suicidal and expressed thoughts of murder. Once taken off the medication, he was prescribed a similar one, marketed under the name Luvox. The medication could well have made his symptoms worse. A study of the chemical fluvoxamine, the active constituent in Luvox, by the Institute for Safe Medication Practices, identified the drug as 8.4 times more likely to be associated with violence than other medications.[123] Harris was later found to have had a therapeutic dose of the drug in his system during the shooting.

In the preceding weeks, Brooks also noticed a change in the boys. He later reported to the FBI that he had 'grown somewhat apart' from the pair. He said, 'Harris and Klebold had been acting a little different … cutting classes and sleeping in class … they had been somewhat more secretive in the last couple of weeks.'[124] On the day of the massacre, his relationship with the boys, albeit a strained one, would ultimately save his life.

On 3 April 1999, Harris' feelings of rejection by his peers at school hit an all-time low. He once again turned to his diary to mete out his feelings. 'I hate you people for leaving me out of so many fun things. And no don't fucking say, 'well that's your fault' because it isn't. You people had my phone # and I asked and all, but no, no no, no don't let the weird looking Eric KID come along. ohh fucking nooo.'[125] Brooks Brown would speculate that Harris felt even more lonely when he was unable to find a date for the prom, while the shy Klebold attended with a female friend. The pair felt like outsiders at school, which was typically hierarchical – at the top were the jocks, noted for wearing white baseball caps, and at the bottom were Harris and Klebold. Klebold wrote about his own rejection by those higher in the pecking order at school: 'You've given us shit for years. You're fucking going to pay for the shit. We don't give a shit, because we're going to die doing it.'[126]

In the late hours of 19 April 1999, the two boys talked to others in an online chat room, perhaps as a cathartic cleansing ahead of the following day. One of them mentioned that 'something bad' was going to happen in Colorado the following day.[127]

The next day, 20 April 1999, was a dark one in American history. For Harris and Klebold, it would usually have commenced with the bowling club, which they would attend from 6am to

7:15am. They were seen in the bowling alley carpark, but did not attend the class. Harris was meant to sit for his Chinese Philosophy test later that day, Brooks Brown was concerned, but not surprised, that Harris had missed the big test. He knew that the teenager's class schedule had become erratic recently.

At 11:10am Harris and Klebold arrived at their school – Columbine High in Littleton, Colorado. Harris parked his car in the junior parking lot and Klebold parked his in the senior one, closest to the school buildings. Both cars were positioned near entrances and exits to the cafeteria, their first target. They were wearing black trousers and boots, black trench coats and T-shirts. Harris' T-shirt had NATURAL SELECTION printed on it. Klebold's T-shirt read WRATH.

Brooks Brown left the school building to have a cigarette and saw Harris getting out of his car. He reminded Harris of the big test they had that day but Harris just looked at him, saying, 'It doesn't matter anymore. Brooks, I like you now. Get out of here. Go home.' Brooks watched as Harris took a duffel bag from the boot of his car. He then wandered away Harris, knowing how strange the teenager had been acting recently. Though Harris had named Brooks as a target, he saved his life by telling him to leave.

By 11:14am, Dylan Klebold and Eric Harris had readied themselves for an onslaught of murder. They were armed with a number of explosive devices, as well as guns and knives. Their bombs ranged from small CO2 containers to 20lb propane gas tank bombs. The smaller devices were designed to detonate via an ignition fuse, while the larger devices were set on timers. The boys planted two 20lb bombs, with timers, in the cafeteria, known as the Commons. Though surveillance cameras were installed in the area, the planting of the bombs was not recorded. The bombs in the Commons were meant to explode at 11:17am, during the lunch A period, when more than a quarter of the school's students took their lunch break.

The boys returned to their cars to await the explosions. Standing at the trunks of their cars, they 'began firing weapons and detonating explosive devices, resulting in the deaths and injuries in numerous students and teachers.'[128] The boys had planned a three-pronged, terrorist-style bombing attack, set to commence with the bombing of the cafeteria, killing all 448 students inside. They also hoped the explosion would bring down the library on the second floor and trap any survivors. They planned to wait at their cars, shooting survivors who tried to escape the rubble, and then to set off explosives in their cars that would kill arriving ambulances and police. The planned attack, however, 'quickly devolved into a forty-nine-minute shooting rampage when the bombs that Harris built fizzled.'[129]

Klebold had written in his diary of his expectations for the attack. 'It will be the most nerve-wracking fifteen minutes of my life after the bombs … seconds will feel like hours.'[130] Already their plan had not gone the way they hoped, although three miles from the school, a diversionary pile of explosives did detonate – a small pipe bomb and aerosol canister caused a large grassfire, which diverted the attention of the fire brigade.

When they realised the bombs inside the school had failed, Harris and Klebold decided to set off on a shooting and explosive spree, armed with two sawn-off shotguns, two 9mm guns and almost 100 smaller incendiary devices. Harris set the timer bombs in the trunks of both of their cars and they prepared to enter the building, intending to take out as many people as they could.

First, they threw a pipe bomb at a group of students near the school's entrance, but the bomb did very little damage. Then a group of students exited through the doors and were met by the two boys in the black trench coats. Seventeen-year-old students Rachel School and Richard Castaldo were the first to be shot. Richard was shot five times; he survived the attack, but was left paralysed. Rachel was shot four times, including one bullet to the head, and was killed.

The two soon realised that their trench coats, worn to hide their weapons, were more of a hindrance than a help. Harris removed his jacket as he headed towards the entrance stairs. Three teenagers, Daniel Rohrbough, Sean Graves and Lance Kirklin, left through the same doors for a cigarette after their lunch break. They saw Harris and Klebold with guns, but assumed they were playing a trick and ignored them. Sixteen-year-old Lance was shot twice, one bullet striking him in the leg and another in the chest. His friend Daniel was struck in the chest. Lance, along with his friend Sean, tried to flee. Lance was shot again in the leg and Sean was hit him in the back and chest. A final shot to his leg stopped him running.

Seeing the carnage, a group of students sitting on the grass near the cafeteria tried to flee, which drew the attention of the shooters. Fifteen-year-old Michael Johnson was shot while running for a nearby lock-up shed. Three other students made it to the sheds uninjured. Mark Taylor, 16, who had been sitting with Michael, was paralysed in the gunfire and remained where he fell, hoping that playing dead would prevent Harris and Klebold from shooting him again.

Seventeen-year-old Anne Marie Hochalter was the next to be wounded. Eating her lunch in the sun with friends, she tried to flee the gunfire, but was shot and paralysed by Harris. The boys threw pipe bombs onto the roof, and fired randomly on students fleeing the scene, without causing any injuries. As they fled, students heard one of the gunmen say, 'This is what we always wanted to do. This is awesome ... Today the world is going to come to an end. Today's the day we die.'[131]

Inside the school, having heard and seen the gunfire, most of the students hid in locked classrooms. Coach Dave Sanders ran through the school, telling students and teachers to hide. His bravery saved the lives of hundreds of students. Calls began filtering in to emergency services.

The injured Sean Graves was crawling to safety when he saw the gunmen heading towards him once more. He rubbed blood from his injuries over his face and played dead as they moved past him. Daniel was not so lucky. Klebold walked over to the fifteen-year-old and shot him dead at point-blank range. Klebold then placed the barrel of his shotgun against the Lance's jaw and fired again; the critically injured boy survived his injuries. The killers stepped on Sean as they headed into the cafeteria, but the wounded teenager did not react to the weight of their boots.

At 11:21am, both boys headed into the cafeteria, which was now empty. They went towards the bombs they had set, wondering why they had not exploded. Meanwhile, a police officer having lunch near the smoking area was the first person to respond to the scene, having received a call that said someone had fallen and was paralysed in the car park.

Walking along the vacant and smoke-filled corridors, the shooters looked from room to room, shooting randomly at walls and lockers and laughing as they stalked for prey. Teacher Patricia 'Patti' Nielson saw the gunfire and assumed it was a prank getting out of hand. Intending to tell them to stop, she went out into the corridor with 17-year-old student Brian Anderson. Stopping at a set of glass doors, she saw Harris raise the gun to chest height. He shot at both of them through the door and their skin was pierced with glass and shrapnel. Patti turned and ran towards the library, where she knew there was a phone. Brian followed.

By then, police had arrived on the scene, but did not enter the building. This decision was later criticised and would eventually see a policy change in how police manage 'live shooters'. They exchanged gunfire with the two gunmen, but remained outside the building.

Several students who tried to flee the school were shot. Seventeen-year-old Stephenie Munson was struck in the ankle, but she continued to run for safety.

Coach Dave Sanders, having locked many students in their classrooms, finally came face to face with Harris and Klebold. He turned away from the shooters and tried to flee, but was shot twice in the neck by Harris. While Harris reloaded his weapon, Klebold dashed past the fallen coach and began shooting down the next corridor towards the cafeteria, before being rejoined by his companion. They spent three minutes shooting along the library corridor and firing off various small explosives into the cafeteria below. Two more bombs were thrown at lockers. Coach Dave Sanders was able to crawl into a nearby room, where students applied first aid treatment in an attempt to save his life. A call to 911 about the coach's injuries was met with an assurance that help was on its way. As the two boys prowled the corridors, they looked into several of the locked science labs, including the one where Dave Sanders was. The students who were giving the teacher first aid hid out of view when the gunmen looked in.

At 11:25am, Patti had made it to the library and warned all students who she found there to hide. Crouching behind the library loans counter, she dialled 911. She remained on the line during the next seven minutes, which would later be described as hell for those inside the library. Fifty-six students were hiding among the desks and shelving in the library, with no way to escape as the shooters headed in their direction.

Fifteen-year-old Evan Todd looked around the corner of a column at the entrance of the library and found Harris staring straight back at him. Harris threw a small pipe bomb at the teenager, which did little damage. Evan looked around the column again and Harris fired several shots at him. The bullets splintered the column, injuring Evan.

Klebold and Harris entered the library. Patti's 911 call gave an accurate recording of what occurred.[132]

Both boys shouted for everyone to get up. Harris called out again, threatening, 'Stand up right now or we'll blow your fucking heads off!' When no one moved, he walked to a desk and yelled,

'Fine. I'll start shooting then.' Klebold shot at 16-year-old special needs student Kyle Velasquez, who was still sitting at one of the computers. He was hit in the back of the head and died instantly. Klebold excitedly exclaimed, 'Woo hoo!'

The shouting and shooting continued. 'All jocks stand up … white baseball cap,' said Klebold, pointing out those who wore the unspoken uniform of the popular kids. No one stood up. Meanwhile, Harris looked out the library window and counted dozens of police cars outside. He called out to Klebold, telling him, 'The pigs are here.' He fired a volley of shots out the window at the cars below.

Klebold moved from desk to desk, firing several shots at Makai Hall, Daniel Steepleton and Patrick Ireland. All three teenagers were injured. Again, he called out, 'Yahoo,' revelling in the harm he was causing at close range. Over the 911 call, Patti Nielson was saying the Lord's Prayer. The dispatcher asked her to stop praying and tell her what was happening. Patti said, 'They're killing kids.' She dropped the phone so she could hide but the line remained open.

Harris pointed his shotgun at 14-year-old Steven Curnow and fired a single shot, killing the boy instantly. He then turned the gun on 17-year-old Kasey Ruegsegger and fired, injuring her. As she moaned in pain, Harris abused the injured woman, saying, 'Stop your bitching, it's merely a flesh wound.'

It was now 11:32am. The press were arriving on the scene. Police remained outside, rescuing those who had fled the buildings.

Harris moved to another area of the library and ducked down under one of the desks, where Cassie Bernall, 17, was hiding. 'Peek-a-boo,' he said, firing at point-blank range and killing her instantly. The kickback from the gun pushed Harris back against the desk behind him. The gun's butt hit him in the face and broke his nose, but he seemed to be unaware that it was bleeding.

Klebold turned the gun on Patrick Ireland, who had been shot moments earlier, but was trying to administer first aid to Makai Hall. He shouted, 'Die … down on the floor,' before shooting him three more times, including two shots to the head, causing critical injuries. Harris then pointed the gun at Bree Pasquale, who begged for her life. Harris told her everyone was going to die and that they were going to blow up the school. He then noticed the blood coming from his nose and turned to Klebold, complaining the gun had hurt him. He walked away from Bree, leaving her to survive the slaughter.

Klebold called out to Harris. 'Reb?' he said, using his online name. 'Hey man, there's a nigger over here.'

Harris answered quickly, 'Shoot him.'

Eighteen-year-old Isiah Shoels begged for his life as Klebold tried to pull him out from under the table. When he was unable to get him out, Harris joined Klebold and fired a shot, killing the young man. Hiding beside Isiah was Matthew Kechter. Klebold aimed the gun at him, and fired, killing him too. Then Harris lit several small pipe bombs and threw them around the library, causing damage to the shelving and structures. He threw one at the area where Makai Hall, Patrick Ireland and Daniel Steepleton were. Makai picked up the bomb and threw it away from them before it exploded.

Seventeen-year-old Mark Kintgen was the next to be injured. Harris fired indiscriminate shots at the shelving before turning the gun on the boy, hitting him in the head and shoulder. Several students who tried to flee as Harris' turned away were then shot. Lisa Kreutz and Valeen Schnurr were struck by a single bullet, then Harris fired again at a group of students, and Lauren Townsend was killed in the gunfire. He fired under more desks and injured 16-year-olds Nicole Nowlen and John Tomlin. As John crawled from beneath the desk, Klebold fired a shot, killing the teenager instantly. He shot at Kelly Fleming, hitting her in the back and killing her, and Jeanna Park, who was with Kelly, was also injured.

As the two gunmen reloaded their guns, Harris spotted John Savage hiding beneath a table. Harris asked the boy to identify himself as Klebold pointed a gun beneath the desk. John told them his name and peered out from his hiding spot. Klebold was an acquaintance of John's. Unsure what else to say, he asked Klebold what he and Harris were doing. Nonchalantly, Klebold responded,

'Oh, just killing people.' John asked if Klebold was going to kill him as well. Klebold shook his head and replied, 'No man, just get out of here, just run … run, run.' At 11:35am, John sprinted from the building, not stopping until he had reached the police line outside.

Harris next turned his gun on 15-year-old Daniel Mauser and shot him in the face, killing him instantly. Then both shooters fired on seventeen-year-olds Corey DePooter, Stephen 'Austin' Eubanks and Jennifer Doyle. All three were injured, before another shot killed Corey.

Complaining that he was out of bullets, Harris considered Klebold's suggestion that they start stabbing people instead. The two killers left the library. They threatened the injured Evan, who was near the door, but did not shoot him. They were heard leaving the library, saying they were heading back to the cafeteria, where they shot at the propane tanks and set off several explosions. At 11:46am, Klebold threw a bomb at the propane tank, causing a fire that made them flee. They fired indiscriminately through several rooms before again returning to the cafeteria to find that the sprinkler system had doused the fire and the larger bombs had still not detonated. The boys were dejected; their grand plan had failed.

At 12:02am, the two killers headed back into the library and started firing at the rescue services outside. Then, at 12:05am, two more shots were heard. Klebold had fired a shot into his left temple and Harris had fired his gun into his mouth. The two had committed suicide after they murdering 13 people and maiming 23 students and teachers. An hour after the attack had begun, SWAT teams and police finally began entering the building. It would take them more than three hours to find all the injured, dying and dead.

Following the shooting many questions were raised regarding the mental stability of the shooters, both teenage killers were seeing psychologists and Harris was taking medication to help him deal with his issues. The medications were blamed by some for his homicidal breakdown. Others were quick to blame violent video games and films, particularly after the killers' references to the film Natural Born Killers was published. Their parents were made to face the world and try and apologise for the killers that they had raised.

Like the friends of Harris and Klebold explained. The two boys, when separate were ok, but when they merged, they were the perfect storm of homicidal rage that enveloped them both. The boys lacked acceptance and understanding from a hierarchical school society and decided to take out their anger on those that they believed wronged them.

John Gacy

John Wayne Gacy Jnr was born to John and Marion Gacy on 17 March 1942. He was the middle child of three siblings, having two sisters, one younger and one older. John Gacy Jnr was adored by his mother but was picked on by his father, who was not impressed by his effeminate son's character. The short, pudgy John was not good at sport—a fact that infuriated his macho, sports-crazy father and became a source of resentment between the two. At school, Gacy was an unexceptional child, doing the bare minimum to scrape through. When he was eleven years old, he fell off a set of swings hitting his head quite hard. After the incident he complained of headaches often and later had several blackout episodes that he blamed on the swing incident.

At the age of sixteen, after a severe fainting episode, he was diagnosed with a blood clot and he also told people that he suffered from a heart condition. Gacy would avoid strenuous activities and spent a great deal of his spare time stealing from local stores or homes. The young man was a compulsive liar and boaster, telling people bizarre tales in an attempt to gain their sympathy or to get something he was after. He left school without graduating and went to a local business college where he found his ability to spin strange stories useful and he succeeded in becoming a successful salesman and, later, a businessman.

Gacy left home after finishing his college certificate and headed to Las Vegas. He was hired as a funeral-home assistant for six months but failed to gain any other significant work, so he returned to the family home in Chicago. By the time he was a young adult, confused about his sexuality, he dated a string of young women before marrying Marilyn Myer in 1964. He got a job working for Marilyn's father at a local Kentucky Fried Chicken and joined the local chapter of the Jaycees.

While at work at the restaurant early in 1967, Gacy chained up one of his young male employees, Edward Lynch, and strangled him into unconsciousness before raping the boy. Edward was fired soon after the attack and went to police to tell them about Gacy. When Gacy was interviewed by police he told them that Edward had been making up the story out of revenge for being fired. The police believed Gacy's story and the matter was forgotten.

In August 1967, Gacy again attacked one of his employees. Fifteen-year-old Donald Vorhees was forced to perform fellatio on his boss after work one evening, but Gacy paid the young boy substantially to silence him before forcing the boy to fellate him several more times. By March 1968, Donald could no longer hide the sexual abuse he was suffering at the hands of Gacy and told his father about the attacks. The pair went to police. Gacy was arrested for the sexual assault of the teenager and was charged on 10 May 1968 with sodomy[133] and sentenced to prison. While in prison, Gacy's wife Marilyn divorced him and the couple never spoke again. On his release, Gacy was again arrested after interfering with a young boy on 12 February 1971. He was charged with disorderly conduct, but when the boy refused to testify the charges were dropped. On 1 January 1972, John Gacy killed for the first time. Gacy wanted to take his mother home around 12.30 a.m. on New Year's Day after a rowdy party. When Mrs Gacy refused, her son left alone. Gacy began prowling the street searching for anyone in the need of company. He eventually picked up a young boy, sixteen-year-old Timothy McCoy from the Greyhound Bus Station at Chicago's Civic Centre. According to Gacy, back at his home the boy attacked him with a knife and Gacy killed him in self-defence. He put the body down into the space under his house. A few days later he buried it there before covering the area with lime.

On 22 June, 1972 Gacy was arrested by police on charges relating to sexual misconduct against another boy, but again the charges were dropped and Gacy continued his sexual conquests. Gacy's second murder victim was 16-year-old John Butkovich. John told his father that he had been underpaid by two weeks by Gacy and was rather bitter with his employer. John's father told him to go and see Gacy and remind him that if he did not correct the pay that he would tell the taxation department about Gacy not paying correct taxes. So, on 31 July 1975, 'Little John' went to see Gacy and the two had an argument. Later that evening, as Gacy cruised the streets for a victim, he spotted John, who was inebriated, getting out of his car at the corner of Sheridan and Lawrence Streets in Chicago. John got into Gacy's car and returned home with him, leaving his car behind. Back at Gacy's house the pair drank alcohol and shared a joint. After showing the boy a magic trick where he was handcuffed, he sodomised the boy and forced him to fellate him. Then Gacy strangled him using a rope as a garrotte. According to Gacy, John had threatened to kill him if he released him from the handcuffs. In a bizarre stretch of the imagination, Gacy believed the killing was justifiable.[134] Once John was dead, Gacy dragged the body to the garage, before retiring for the few remaining hours of darkness. The next day Gacy spent his time digging a ditch in a corner of the garage floor. Once he had dug quite a large hole he dragged the rigid body of John Butkovich into it. There, 'Little John' Butkovich's body remained until after Gacy's arrest in December 1978.

On 6 April 1976, Gacy killed his third victim, Darrell Sampson. The young man had accompanied Gacy back to his home, possibly with the lure of a job and a bit of a party. Darrell was raped and abused before being strangled by Gacy.

On 14 May 1976, a little over five weeks after the murder of Darrell Sampson, Randall Reffett and Samuel Stapleton both disappeared. Randall was the first to disappear, with Gacy picking the boy up in broad daylight and taking him to his home, where he was subjected to acts of sexual abuse and violence. Fourteen-year-old Sam Stapleton was walking home from his sister's house at 11 p.m. that same night when he was also picked up. The boy had been only a block from his own house when Gacy pulled up beside him and offered him a lift. Gacy took the boy instead to his house where the teenager was strangled and raped. Both Randall and Sam were interred in the same grave under Gacy's house.

Gacy's next victim luckily survived being attacked by the killer. Sixteen-year-old Mike Rossi met John Gacy on 22 May 1976. The pair spent the night at Gacy's home, drinking and smoking drugs. The following day, Gacy threw Mike to the ground, sat on the boy's chest and forced his penis into the young man's mouth, demanding that Mike perform fellatio on him. For some reason, Gacy did not kill the boy. Mike never reported the attack to the police and continued to visit Gacy at his home. He was given a job by the killer and threatened with the sack if he ever told anyone about the attack. Later, Mike moved in with Gacy, and after the killer's arrest became a suspect in some of the killings.

Seventeen-year-old Michael Bonin told his mother he was going to help a friend with a painting job on 3 June 1976. The painting job was for Gacy, and after the young man had finished work for the day he went home with the older man for a few drinks.

He was never seen alive again. Later, after the killer's arrest, several of Michael's personal items were found in Gacy's possession.

On 10 June 1976, teenager William 'Billy' Carroll Jnr was working part time as a prostitute when he was picked up by Gacy and taken to the killer's home. Once alone in the house, Gacy raped and tortured the boy before strangling him to death. Billy was then pushed down into the crawlspace under Gacy's house, where he joined the other six bodies in various stages of decomposition.

The eighth murder victim was 18-year-old Rick Johnson on 6 August 1976. His mother dropped him off at concert on the other side of Chicago that evening. He told her that he would find his own way home as several of his friends were going to be at the concert and he would catch a lift home with them. The killer saw Rick heading away from the concert alone and offered him a ride. As he had done so often before, Gacy took the boy home where he tied him up, raped him and killed him, burying him away from the others in the floor under the laundry.

Nineteen-year-old David Cram was luckier than most. He was able to escape from Gacy. The young man moved into Gacy's house in August 1976 after starting work at his construction company, PDM, the previous month. On 11 August 1976, after spending the day celebrating his birthday, David returned to Gacy's house where he was attacked. Gacy did not expect the young man to be strong, yet even with his arms cuffed behind his back David was able to overpower Gacy by shoulder-charging him and escaping. The would-be victim later committed suicide.[135]

On Saturday 11 December 1976, 17-year-old Gregory Godzik had been on a date with his girlfriend Judy. After dropping Judy home, Greg decided to visit his boss, John Gacy, at home. Gacy opened his front door and happily invited Greg inside. Gacy plied the young man with alcohol before deciding to show Greg the rope trick he used in his clown act at various hospitals. Gacy tied Greg's hands behind his back. Gacy then grabbed Greg around the throat and squeezed. He watched the boy pass out, helpless against Gacy and the ropes around his wrists. The killer then sexually abused Greg for hours before strangling him and reviving him, over and over again, before finally killing him. Greg's body was pushed down into the crawlspace.

Gacy murdered 19-year-old John Szyc on 20 January 1977. Gacy picked up the young man at Bughouse Nightclub. After having sex, Szyc was bound by Gacy and strangled.

It was less than two months after the murder of John Szyc that Gacy murdered again. Victim eleven was 20-year-old Jon Prestige. Jon Prestige had been feeling bored on the evening of 15 March 1977, and told his flatmate that he was going to head to the Bughouse, a place he had heard about from friends. This was the place where John Szyc also disappeared. Jon had been enjoying himself at the nearby nightclub when he accepted an offer from

Gacy of a party at his house. Gacy offered the young man drugs and free alcohol to go with him. So Jon happily agreed and like many of the young men before him, did not leave Gacy's home alive. The young man's body was the first to be exhumed after Gacy's arrest during Christmas 1978.

The twelfth victim of John Gacy was 19-year-old Matthew Bowman. The young man had been dropped off by his mother at a Chicago railway station on 5 July 1977. Moments later, Gacy arrived and offered the young man a lift. Matthew got into Gacy's car and was driven back to Gacy's home. Once inside the house, Matthew was drugged, raped and sexually abused before being strangled to death and buried under the house with the others.

Robert Gilroy met Gacy a little over two months after the murder of Matthew Bowman. The eighteen-year-old had set off on 15 September 1977 to meet with friends for a horse-riding trip when he was picked up by Gacy. The young man died after hours of sexual torture. On 25 September 1977, 19-year-old John Mowery became the fourteenth known victim. On the day of his murder John had gone to visit his mother. Gacy offered him a ride. Gacy drove the nineteen-year-old to his own house. Repeating his usual murderous routine, he tied the young man up and raped him before strangling him to death and putting the remains with the others in his crawlspace.

The next victim was 21-year-old Russell Nelson on 17 October 1977. The man had been out at a disco on the night of his murder when Gacy offered him a lift home. Once at the Gacy home, he too was murdered and buried in the crawlspace under the killer's home. Robert Winch, a sixteen-year-old, had run away from Kalamazoo, Michigan and was picked up by Gacy on 11 November 1977 and taken back to the killer's house. Robert was systematically raped and strangled until he died. He was interred with the other bodies in the rapidly filling crawlspace of Gacy's home where he remained for thirteen months.

The killings were escalating and the next victim was murdered on 18 November 1977, only a week after Robert Winch. The seventeenth known victim of Gacy was 20-year-old Tommy Baling. Gacy offered him a ride. Tommy accepted the lift and ended up at Gacy's home. Tommy was subjected to various sex acts before being shown Gacy's rope trick, where he was strangled to death as he struggled against the loops around his wrists and throat. Like the others, Tommy was buried in the graveyard under Gacy's house.

The next to die was 19-year-old marine David Talsma on 9 December 1977. Gacy took the man home where he was raped and strangled and buried under the house with the others. By the end of 1977, as the victim tally continued to grow, Gacy was diagnosed with syphilis.

Around 30 December 1977 another victim escaped with his life. Nineteen-year-old Robert Donnell was picked by Gacy. According to Gacy, he propositioned the young man, offering money to accompany him home. Robert agreed and Gacy drove to his house. Until morning, Gacy raped and sodomised Robert using dildos. Gacy also tied up Robert and whipped him with chains. Gacy pushed the man's head into the water filled bath and held his head under until Robert stopped fighting and loss consciousness. Gacy then revived the victim and started the torture again. He urinated on his victim and also held a gun to Robert's head and spun the barrel, firing when it stopped, playing the sick game of Russian Roulette. The torture continued for eight hours. For some unknown reason, Gacy decided not to kill the nineteen-year-old. He drove to the street where he had picked up his victim and dumped the man, bruised and battered on the side of the road. Robert memorised the number plate and stumbled to the police station to report the attack. A week later, on 6 January 1978 Gacy was arrested for the brutal attack on Robert, yet after interviewing the killer the officers believed Gacy's side of the story and he was released.

The nineteenth known victim, Billy Kindred, was not as lucky as Robert. He was last seen on 16 February 1978 by his fiancé. Billy found himself in Gacy's torture house, handcuffed and begging for his life as he was beaten and raped by Gacy. Like the other victims, Billy's body was interred in the crawlspace the next morning, when Gacy had finished with him.

On 21 March 1978, Jeff Rignall stormed out of the apartment he shared with his girlfriend. Gacy pulled up beside the twenty-six-year-old and offered him a ride. Once Gacy had Jeff inside the car, he lit up a marijuana joint and the two men shared it. As Jeff relaxed, Gacy pounced, grabbing the man around the head and shoving a chloroform-soaked cloth over Jeff's nose and mouth. Jeffrey woke inside Gacy's home, his head buzzing. Gacy raped Jeff, then pushed the rag with chloroform over the man's face again to render him unconscious repeatedly before waking him each time to sexually abuse him, screaming 'you love it' each time he did.[136] Jeff was woken a final time near the street where he had first encountered the killer. The man, though battered and disoriented, made his way home before being taken to the hospital and then the police station.

The police believed the man's story—his battered and swollen face testament to what he had told them—however he was unable to give a clear description of his attacker nor the location of the assault. Police were helpless to do anything. Jeff decided to take the matter into his own hands. He sat on the side of the road where Gacy had picked him up and waited in the hope that Gacy would again drive by. Though unsure of the number plate, Jeff did remember that it was a vanity plate with only three letters on it.

Finally, Gacy drove past Jeff. The man knew it was his attacker and wrote down the number plate—PDM—and took it to the police. He was certain his attacker would face justice. Yet as time went on and Jeff was not called to provide further testimony or evidence he knew that nothing had been done. Like the other boys who had told police about Gacy his report was noted but not followed up nor investigated.

One of the final victims was Tim O'Rourke. He remained nameless for quite some time after his body was discovered. It was only through a tattoo that Gacy remembered who the boy was. Tim met Gacy around 14 June 1978 and was never seen alive again. The young man had left his apartment to buy cigarettes when Gacy made him a better offer of free marijuana at his home. The boy with the 'Tim Lee' tattoo gladly accepted the killers' offer and returned with Gacy. Like the others, Tim was raped and abused before being strangled to death. Yet this time he was not buried in the cemetery underneath Gacy's home. The crawlspace was now full of up to thirty bodies; the smell in the confined space was unimaginable; the stench of decaying bodies emanating through the floorboards of Gacy's house. So now Gacy had to find another graveyard. Tim's body was wrapped in a tarp and thrown into the Des Plaines River from one of the bridges along Highway I55.

The next victim was also thrown into the Des Plaines River. Nineteen-year-old Frank Landingin, a part-time male prostitute, argued with his girlfriend on the night of 3 November 1978. The argument continued into the early hours of the next morning and by 2 a.m. on 4 November 1978 Frank stormed out of the house and headed into the night and into the clutches of John Gacy. He was taken back to the house of horrors and raped and tortured for several hours before finally being strangled by Gacy.

The penultimate victim was 20-year-old James Mazzara who met his death in November 1978. The young man had been out looking for a new place to rent when he found himself on the doorstep of Gacy's home. He was ushered inside the house and shown around. Soon the scene turned ugly and James found himself bound and gagged. The killer raped the young man several times during which James was choked to death on his own underpants that had been shoved down his throat.

Robert Piest was a handsome young man with the long flowing hair. The evening he disappeared was Monday 11 December 1978. Robert was working at the Nisson Pharmacy in Des Plaines when John Gacy walked into the store. He had come to discuss with the owner a refitting of the pharmacy. The boy, with his mother waiting outside to pick him after his shift, went to see Gacy before he left. Gacy told the boy to get into the car to discuss a job and then leaned over towards the young man and clamped a cloth with chloroform on it over Rob's mouth. He had later tied a rope around the young boy's throat and twisted it twice to kill him.[137]

Being the last person to see Rob alive, Gacy was the prime suspect from the beginning and after he invited police into his home to look around, the stench of death told them there was something going on. One officer went down into the crawlspace and dug around in the soft earth where he quickly found a decomposed foot. Before he was arrested, Gacy confided in his business associate Ronald Rhode. He told the man, 'Ron, I've been a bad boy, I killed thirty people, give or take a few'.[138] Within two days,[139] officers charged Gacy with murder, unaware of how many counts would be part of the final tally. However, Gacy was ready for them with an insanity defence. He began talking about 'Bad Jack' who hated homosexuals as well as other personas.

On 22 December 1978, Gacy was furious when he learnt that the officers were pulling apart his immaculate house to get to the crawlspace. He asked for a pen and paper and drew them a map of where the bodies were buried, so they would not destroy his home. The map was accurate, and though it did not prevent the officers from completely removing the floor from Gacy's house, it did give the prosecution an exact map to overlay to pinpoint the locations of the bodies recovered, that then cemented Gacy's guilt at trial.

In total twenty-eight bodies were removed from the crawlspace of Gacy's home. The body of John Butkovich was dug up from under the garage concrete floor and Rick Johnson's body was discovered under the laundry room. Three others, Tim

O'Rourke, James Mazarra and Robert Piest were recovered from the waters of the Des Plaines River.

The trial of John Gacy opened in the Cook County Court on 6 February 1980. By 12 March 1980 the trial had come to its conclusion and after two hours the seven men and five women of the jury handed their decision to the judge. Gacy was found guilty of all thirty-three murders and the following day he was sentence to death by lethal injection. While in prison, Gacy gave numerous interviews. In one, he was disgusted that that the media grouped him in with other serial killers, saying, 'Whether it's Berkowitz, whether it's Bundy, whether it's Williams, Wayne Williams down in Atlanta, or Charlie Manson, God I hate that when they put they put me in the same club as them'.[140]

At midnight on 11 May 1994 Gacy became the 100th person to be executed in Illinois, his final words were 'Kiss my Ass'. At 12.58 a.m. he was pronounced dead.

Endnotes

[1] 'A loving letter from a mother', *Sydney Morning Herald,* March 4, 1987
[2] Based on author's conversations with David Birnie (2005).
[3] ibid
[4] ibid
[5] ibid
[6] ibid
[7] ibid
[8] ibid
[9] 'Sex shock confession', *Sydney Morning Herald,* November 16, 1986
[10] Based on the author's conversations with David Birnie (2005).
[11] R v Birnie.
[12] 'No remorse by killer says judge', *Sydney Morning Herald,* March 4, 1987
[13] ibid
[14] Douglas Adams, *Hitchhikers Guide to the Galaxy: a Trilogy in Four Parts.*
[15] Conversations between the author and the subject 2001-2018
[16] Bingham, M. 1996 Suddenly One Sunday
[17] R v Bryant (22 November 1996)
[18] ibid
[19] ibid
[20] Bingham, M. 1996 Suddenly One Sunday
[21] R v Bryant (22 November 1996)
[22] ibid
[23] ibid
[24] ibid
[25] ibid
[26] ibid
[27] The Childhood of a serial killer documentary
[28] Ben Lawson et al Ted Bundy – serial killer timelines
[29] The Childhood of a serial killer documentary
[30] The Childhood of a serial killer documentary
[31] Katherine Ramsland, *Imagining Ted Bundy* Psychology Today
[32] Katherine Ramsland, *Imagining Ted Bundy* Psychology Today
[33] Kevin M Sullivan The Bundy Murders : A Comprehensive History
[34] Stephen G. Michaud, Hugh Aynesworth, *The Only Living Witness*
[35] Stephen G. Michaud, Hugh Aynesworth, *The Only Living Witness*
[36] Stephen G. Michaud, Hugh Aynesworth, *The Only Living Witness*
[37] Stephen G. Michaud, Hugh Aynesworth, *The Only Living Witness*
[38] The Childhood of a serial killer documentary
[39] The Childhood of a serial killer documentary, Dr Dobson
[40] P27 Wansell, G. *An Evil Love: The Life of Frederick West* Headline (1996)

[41] Fred West, Wikipedia (accessed July 2007)

[42] P73 Wansell, G. *An Evil Love: The Life of Frederick West* Headline (1996)

[43] P73 Wansell, G. *An Evil Love: The Life of Frederick West* Headline (1996)

[44] Fred had confessed and recanted the confession to Mary's murder multiple times.

[45] P85 Wansell, G. *An Evil Love: The Life of Frederick West* Headline (1996)

[46] P89 Wansell, G. *An Evil Love: The Life of Frederick West* Headline (1996)

[47] Mae was born May June West on June 1, 1972

[48] P 107 Wansell, G. *An Evil Love: The Life of Frederick West* Headline (1996)

[49] P129 Wansell, G. *An Evil Love: The Life of Frederick West* Headline (1996)

[50] P138 Wansell, G. *An Evil Love: The Life of Frederick West* Headline (1996)

[51] P143 Wansell, G. *An Evil Love: The Life of Frederick West* Headline (1996)

[52] P395 Masters, Brian *She Must Have Known* Corgi (1997)

[53] P158 Wansell, G. *An Evil Love: The Life of Frederick West* Headline (1996)

[54] P395 Masters, Brian *She Must Have Known* Corgi (1997)

[55] P395 Masters, Brian *She Must Have Known* Corgi (1997)

[56] P189 Wansell, G. *An Evil Love: The Life of Frederick West* Headline (1996)

[57] P196 Wansell, G. *An Evil Love: The Life of Frederick West* Headline (1996)

[58] Howard Ogden, *Fred and Rose: The West Murders* Channel 5 Documentary, England

[59] *Fred and Rose: The West Murders* Channel 5 Documentary, England

[60] Fred West's own words *Fred and Rose: The West Murders* Channel 5 Documentary, England

[61] Fred West's own words *Fred and Rose: The West Murders* Channel 5 Documentary, England

[62] Fred West's own words *Fred and Rose: The West Murders* Channel 5 Documentary, England

[63] Fred West's own words *Fred and Rose: The West Murders* Channel 5 Documentary, England

[64] Fred West's own words *Fred and Rose: The West Murders* Channel 5 Documentary, England

[65] p12 Wansell, G. *An Evil Love: The Life of Frederick West* Headline (1996)

[66] Fred West's own words *Fred and Rose: The West Murders* Channel 5 Documentary, England

[67] Fred West's own words *Fred and Rose: The West Murders* Channel 5 Documentary, England

[68] Fred West's own words *Fred and Rose: The West Murders* Channel 5 Documentary, England

[69] Fred West's own words *Fred and Rose: The West Murders* Channel 5 Documentary, England

[70] *Fred and Rose: The West Murders* Channel 5 Documentary, England

[71] *Fred and Rose: The West Murders* Channel 5 Documentary, England

[71] Decca Aitkenhead I'm so like my dad, says Stephen West,

[72] Bruce MacFarlan, 'Horrific Video Tapes As Evidence: Balancing Open Court And Victims' Privacy', *Criminal Law Quarterly* 413, 1999

[73] Williams, Stephen, *Invisible Darkness,* Bantam Books, 1998

[74] ibid

[75] Bernardo and Homolka case, http://bernardo-homolka.tumblr.com/.

[76] Stephen Williams, *Invisible Darkness,* Bantam Books, 1998

[77] Peter Vronsky, *Female Serial Killers: How and Why Women Become Monsters*, Berkley Books, 2007

[78] 'Bernardo sentenced to life', *Kingman Daily Miner,* September 3, 1995

[79] 'Man sentenced to life in prison for 2 deaths', *Lakeland Ledger,* September 2, 1995

[80] 'Man convicted in sex slayings', *The Freelance Star,* September 1, 1995

[81] 'Bernardo admits to raping 14 women', *Lakeland Ledger,* November 4, 1995.

[82] 'Killer of 2 Canadian girls sentenced', *Pittsburgh Post Gazette,* September 2, 1995

[83] 'Town destroys house of horrors', *Reading Eagle,* December 7, 1995.

[84] T vs The United Kingdom – 24724/94 [1999] ECHR 170

[85] Shirley Lynn Scott The Murder of James Bulger, Court TV

[86] Stephen Wright et al Revealed: the horror image drawn by Jon Venables just weeks before he killed James Bulger. Daily Mail

[87] ibid

[88] ibid

[89] V vs The United Kingdom – 24888/94 [1999] ECHR 171

[90] T vs The United Kingdom – 24724/94 [1999] ECHR 170

[91] V vs The United Kingdom – 24888/94 [1999] ECHR 171

[92] V vs The United Kingdom – 24888/94 [1999] ECHR 171

[93] Ralph Bulger *My James*

[94] Ralph Bulger *My James*

[95] T vs The United Kingdom – 24724/94 [1999] ECHR 170

[96] Most Evil – Murderous Women Documentary

[97] John Poersch, *Marybeth Tinning She is a wicked woman*

[98] John Poersch, *Marybeth Tinning She is a wicked woman*

[99] Most Evil – Murderous Women Documentary

[100] Robert Boorstin, *Schenectady Child Suffocation Case Goes to Jury* New York Times 16.07.87

[101] Robert Gavin, *Rare Glimpse into child killer's mind* Times Union 11.02.11

[102] Most Evil – Murderous Women Documentary

[103] James Leggett, *Grand Jury Investigating Deaths of At Least Two Tinning Children* Schenectady Gazette 18.06.86

[104] Radford University Serial Killer Timelines: Marybeth Tinning

[105] Most Evil – Murderous Women Documentary

[106] Radford University Serial Killer Timelines: Marybeth Tinning

[107] Radford University Serial Killer Timelines: Marybeth Tinning

[108] Joyce Egginton, *From the Cradle to the Grave* Mass Market 1990

[109] Radford University Serial Killer Timelines: Marybeth Tinning

[110] Most Evil – Murderous Women Documentary

[111] James Leggett, *Grand Jury Investigating Deaths of At Least Two Tinning Children* Schenectady Gazette 18.06.86

[112] John Poersch, *Marybeth Tinning She is a wicked woman*

[113] Robert Gavin, *Rare Glimpse into child killer's mind* Times Union 11.02.11

ERIC HARRIS AND DYLAN KLEBOLD

[114] Eric Harris diary entry

[115] Jeffrey Kluger Brothers in Arms: Sibling Pyschology and the Bombing Suspects http://science.time.com/2013/04/19/siblings/

[116] Jeffrey Kluger Brothers in Arms: Sibling Pyschology and the Bombing Suspects http://science.time.com/2013/04/19/siblings/

[117] Jeffrey Kluger Brothers in Arms: Sibling Pyschology and the Bombing Suspects http://science.time.com/2013/04/19/siblings/

[118] Dave Cullen, *Columbine,* p32

[119] Eric Harris and Dylan Klebold – Referenced in Criminal Minds

[120] Dylan Klebold Diary entry

[121] REB Doomed – Eric Harris' online AOL blog

[122] Zero Hour: Columbine Documentary

[123] Moore TJ, Glenmullen J, Furberg CD (2010) Prescription Drugs Associated with Reports of Violence Towards Others. PLoS ONE 5(12): e15337. doi:10.1371/journal.pone.0015337

[124] FBI Columbine High School File

[125] Eric Harris Diary entry

[126] Dylan Klebold Diary entry

[127] FBI Columbine High School File

[128] FBI Columbine High School File

[129] Greg Topp *10 years later, the real story behind Columbine* USA Today 14.04.2009

[130] Dylan Klebold diary entry

[131] Wayne Bennett *Criminal Investigation P 345*

[132] Available from various online sources, see youtube for actual recordings

CHARLES MANSON

[133] An interesting fact is that a charge of sodomy in Iowa includes oral sex

[134] People v. Gacy, 468 N.E.2d 1171 (Ill. 1984).

[135] 'Death toll rises', *Chicago Tribune,* August 12, 2001

[136] People v. Gacy, 468 N.E.2d 1171 (Ill. 1984).

[137] ibid

[138] ibid

[139] Gacy v. Welborn 61 USLW 2665

[140] 'Top 50 serial killer moments', YouTube documentary, http://www.youtube.com/watch?v=qNtTeuXHwew .

Printed in Great Britain
by Amazon